the dateable rules

a guide to the sexes

Guys Side!

Justin Lookadoo
and Hayley Morgan

Hungry Planet

Fleming H. Revell

A Division of Baker Book House Co
Grand Rapids, Michigan 49516

Published by the same cool people who also brought you "DATEABLE"

— both Dateable & Dateable Rules have been pre-doodled for your convenience

Interior design by Brian Bruastiga

Table of Contents
FOR GUYS

NO Girls Allowed!

The Owner's Manual

This is a book. But it's more than one book—it's really two books glued together and sold as one book. It doesn't get any better than that! Unless of course you live in a grass hut in Hawaii and play in the ocean all day. That's pretty cool too. But getting back to our book, we call it Flip. Well, really we call it a flip book, but you can call it Flip for short. That means **one side** is written **for girls** and the **other** is written **for guys.** For those of you who are already confused, that means that if you pee standing up, you're reading the right side.

To help you better utilize your two books in one, we have provided these easy-to-follow directions in both English and Japanese. (We really don't know Japanese, but what's an owner's manual without it?) Make sure you have all of the parts required to operate this book before proceeding. See the list of parts below:

- Book
- Pen (not included)
- Bible (not included)
- Vital information (partially included)
- Focus Group Members (not included)
- Date Night (ideas included, date not included)
- Blank spaces (provided for your writing pleasure)

- 本
- ペン (含まれません)
- 聖書 (含まれません)
- 重要な情報 (一部含まれます)
- フォーカス・グループ・メンバー (含まれません)
- デート・ナイト (アイディアは含まれますが相手は含まれません)
- 余白スペース (自由にお書きください)

Follow these simple steps to maximize your *Dateable Rules* experience:

1. Read the book. If that's too vague, don't worry—you can resort to the "How to Read This Book" directions at the beginning of each week. If you decide not to follow the HRTB directions, then please finish the week by the end of the week.

1. 初めに言ったはずです。本を読んでください。次に、前文をもう一度読んでください。

2. Underline things. Underlining is good, unless of course you're a member of the ICA (Ink Conservationists Association). But since they don't date, they probably aren't reading this book. In any case, underlining will help you quickly locate and distribute information to the guys you are doing the book with.

2. まだがんばって読もうしてるのですか。これは教科書ではなく、デートに関する本なんです。訳そうなんて無駄な努力はやめて、実践してください。

3. Date Night. It's the night you date. You date either the girl or the group of girls you are doing this book with. Hmm, that sounded completely wrong. Let me rephrase: Date Night is a night for everyone who is doing the book together to get together and go out, whether it's a couple or a whole group. Be sure to read all the articles for that week before advancing to Date Night. The goal of the Date Night will all become clear by then.

3. まだ訳しているようですね。もう3つ目。そろそろデート・ナイトに移ってもいいのでは？さあ、がんばって！

4. Focus Group. The Focus Group happens on the final day of the week. Please refer to "Legal Mumbo Jumbo" (it's not hard to find; it's on the next page) for more information on the purpose of said Focus Group. Basically it's a group of people who get together to talk. That's all we have to say about that for now.

4. おめでとう。この本にあるすべての日本語の翻訳に成功しました。もちろん最後の文節を訳したとしたら大間違い。最初に戻って、もう一度がんばってください。

Important Safety Tips

To reduce the risk of electrical shock, never read this book while operating a toaster while taking a bath.

4 out of 5 dentists surveyed didn't read this book but did recommend brushing with fluoride toothpaste twice daily to prevent tooth decay.

Do not read this book while driving a motorized vehicle or operating heavy machinery.

Kickoff Focus Group

Legal Mumbo Jumbo

Sprite was getting its butt kicked in the soda war. Its sales were crashing and burning, and the company wanted to know why. **Those guys who should have been buying their stuff—their "target audience"—weren't buying it.** So the brains at the company came up with a brilliant idea. To **find out what their target audience wanted,** they decided to ask them, "So what would make a soft drink cool? What would make you drink our flavored water over theirs?"

To do this they hired a firm to do **focus groups** for them. This company's deal was to get a bunch of the target audience together to talk about why they don't drink Sprite and what would make them change their minds. Once they figured out what teenage guys wanted, they made Sprite look like the answer to their soft drink prayers. Ingenious.

Today Sprite is one of the best-selling soft drinks on the market. Thank goodness for focus groups.

Wouldn't it be cool if you could **do a focus group on *your* "target audience"—girls**? To get in their heads? To figure out what their words really mean? Well, dream no more. Today your dream has become a reality. Before you lift another *Dateable* finger, you're gonna do a little **focus group of your own.** You guys and your target audience, the girls you do this study with, will get to ask each other questions—like why guys are so cool and girls are so crazy (or something like that). You are going to get together and focus before you go any further in the book. If you are doing this study with your crush, you're gonna find out some stuff about each other that you never understood.

What do chicks want? My my, don't we all want to know. So to get started, guys, you are going to take a little quiz to see how well you understand girls. Then you'll take 5 minutes as a group to **write down <u>5 things you want to know about girls.</u>** And, you guessed it, the girls are going to be able to ask you 5 things they've always wanted to know about you. Nothing's sacred.

7

s group • kickoff focus group • kickoff focus group • kickoff focus group • kickoff focus group • kickoff focus group • kickoff focus g

Ask anything: "Why are you so moody?" "What do you look for in a guy?" "What's a good way to ask you out?" Stuff that you've always wanted to ask but been too afraid to. (Duh Note: If there are 30 of you doing this focus group, you still only get to ask 5 questions. Get it? Too many people. Too many questions. Too little time. Choose the best ones.)

Now, once you've got your Qs, it's time for the Q&A part of the Focus Group. If it's just you and your **girlfriend,** get somewhere quiet and go through the questions. **If you're a group,** then here's your deal: Get all the guys on one side of the room facing the girls, who are on the other side of the room. **Get a moderator,** someone who can read the questions and **run the timer.** Each side gets up to **5 minutes to answer each question.** That's the limit. For some questions it might only take a sec, but for others there will be lots of yappin' once the answer comes out. **Get a dry-erase board** or something else to make your notes on. (It can serve as evidence in the lawsuits you might end up bringing against each other.)

At the end of your time, you will have what focus groups for MTV and Coca-Cola pay thousands of dollars for: a real slice of Americana. The truth about the opposite sex—or is it?

Dateable BASH PLAN

Okay, we're jumping way ahead here, but we have to, because in the last Focus Group you are going to get your party on. It's going to be the *Dateable* Bash. But to make it happen, you have to start doing things now. Like today. So before you begin the journey, you're going to see how the story ends so you can plan the final blowout.

Here's the breakdown to get you rolling.

8

The *Dateable* Bash Planning Team: At the end of this book, you're going to get to throw a party. But we all know it takes time to plan a good party. So today we're going to get teams together so the party will hop and not flop. After you've done your quiz, brainstorming, and Q&A, you're going to assign teams. You need to pick a News Crew, Award Team, Design Team, Party Team, and any other teams you think will help. These are the people who are going to pull this whole event together. If just you and your crush are doing this book, then you guys might only document the month with your journals and your cameras and then have a big dinner or some kind of get-together to remember your month.

Descrip of Each Team:

News Crew – On the last day of this adventure (i.e., at the end of this book), the News Crew will take you for a walk down memory lane. From news reports of the month to video footage and slide shows, the News Crew's job is to record the memories for everyone involved. This team can be any size and involve any number of jobs. Just a few to choose from are written below. Pick your team and then brainstorm about who will do what throughout the month. Also start to figure out how you will present your report on the last day. **Members of the News Crew:**

Anchor – This person will be the talking head. The one who will get up in front of everyone and lead the recap. You can play with this. Get a male and female and do it like *SNL* news or the *Today* show. Or just get one person to do it. Your job will be to take quotes, record events, and put together a heartfelt/funny presentation for your group using all the cool info the rest of the Crew gets over the month.

9

Photog – This person is in charge of pics. Take 'em during the week, on Date Night, and during Focus Groups. Get all the action shots you can.

Videographer – Name says it all. Shoot the month. Catch people talking about Date Night, dating, focusing, all the stuff you will be doing throughout the month.

Writer – Writers write. Beautiful how that works, isn't it? So the writer for this project will take notes on everything that happens. Maybe write it like a journal or like a TV show. But keep track of the things that go on in your group and the stuff that people say.

Awards Team – This team's job is to figure out what kinds of awards will be given out at the *Dateable* Bash. Shop 'til you drop. Find small things that can be given to the people who will be voted for. Make a list of things people can win: "Most Dateable," "Most Improved Dater," "Most Likely to Get the Door for a Girl," "Most Likely to Shut Up and Be Mysterious," "Best Planner," "Best Complimentor." The list could go on and on. Your job is to decide on the awards, make ballots for everyone, figure out what prizes each winner will get, and set up for voting to take place on *Dateable* Bash night.

Design Team – This team's job can include any number of things. Create a photo album using the photos taken. Make a slide show and put it to music. Create poster boards to decorate the walls. Hang banners from the ceiling. Make the night memorable. Decorate away!

Party Team – If you're going to have a party, someone has to plan. This team's job is to make sure the party happens. Find drinks, food, music, whatever. Make the night a big bash. Find the location, band, actors, games, whatever you need to make the night a blast. Make sure that you coordinate with the News Crew so that they have everything they need as far as electrical

10

outlets, video screens, tables, and so on. Your job is really to coordinate everyone so that you all work together as one big team. You come up with the flow for the night. Figure out what happens when. Get with the Design Team to see what they need. Yep, you are the traffic cop of the deal.

This is all about the fun. When you make it through the book, you will deserve a party. It will be the perfect ending to your journey through *Dateability*.

So here's the plan for this *Dateable* Kickoff:

Quiz Time: "Do You Understand Girls?" (5 minutes)

Brainstorm: Come up with 5 questions you want to ask the girls (5 minutes)

Q&A: Girls and guys take turns asking each other the 5 questions (total 50 minutes max)

Dateable **Bash Party Planning**

Got it? Okay then, get crackin'. Take the "Do You Understand Girls?" quiz below and score your answers. It'll help you see what kind of questions you need to ask the girls.

Quiz: Do you Understand Girls?

1. When you start liking a girl, you:
   a. call her on the phone just to talk
   b. tell her friend you like her
   c. just pray that she will get the hint and ask you out

2. At a party you:
   a. find all your guy friends and make a wild night of it
   b. find the girl you like and make conversation with her
   c. sit on the couch like the lone wolf, waiting for the girl you like to find you and talk to you

11

3. When you see a girl carrying a big box, you:
    a. drop everything to go help her carry it
    b. just watch her walk by. I mean, girls are just as strong as guys, so why should you help her?
    c. ask her if she needs a hand

4. If you saw two cute girls sitting together at a lunch table, you would:
    a. walk up and ask if you could join them
    b. go sit somewhere else where you could see them
    c. sit at their table but not say anything to them

5. When you take a girl home from a date, you:
    a. get out of the car and walk her to her front door
    b. let her out while you stay in the car and wait 'til she's safely inside
    c. let her out and drive off before she even gets to the front door

6. If you are dating a girl, you:
    a. think it's okay to date other girls too. I mean, you aren't married to anyone.
    b. think it's only cool to date one girl at a time
    c. talk to other girls on the phone but only technically date one girl at a time

7. On Valentine's Day, for the girl you like you prefer to:
    a. try not to think about it 'cuz it's a girl holiday
    b. buy her a card and some flowers
    c. Valentine's Day? Who gives a rip!

8. When you are dating a girl, you most like to:
    a. put love notes in her locker
    b. buy her flowers
    c. hang out with her, but none of that mushy stuff like cards and flowers

9. If a girl you don't really want to have for a girlfriend is flirting with you, you:
    a. treat her badly so she'll stop making a fool of herself

12

b. ask her out. At least she's a girl and she'll go out with you.
c. tell her you appreciate the fact that she likes you but you just aren't interested in her like that

10. When it comes to talking, you:
   a. prefer not to talk much. It's just so boring.
   b. think communication is important, so you make lots of effort to talk with your girlfriends
   c. talk everyone's ear off. You have lots of opinions about lots of stuff, and you aren't afraid to share them.

Time to get your score: Add up all your points:

1. a = 1, b = 2, c = 3	6. a = 3, b = 1, c = 3
2. a = 3, b = 1, c = 3	7. a = 3, b = 1, c = 3
3. a = 1, b = 3, c = 2	8. a =1, b = 1, c = 3
4. a = 1, b = 3, c = 2	9. a =3, b = 3, c = 1
5. a = 1, b = 2, c = 3	10. a =3, b = 1, c = 2

10–13: Girl Power. *You've got it. Girls, that is. You've got them figured out. You must be a girl magnet. Or you just got lucky on this stupid quiz. Either way, don't get too cocky. You'll never truly understand women, 'cuz if you did, we'd have to kill you.*

14–23: Bookworm. *The books are open and you've read a few pages, but you still have tons to learn about women. You are on the way to success, though, so keep it up. Girls will be on you like stink on a pig! Keep on keepin' on.*

24–30: Clueless one. *Join the rest of the male population in being clueless about women. Don't sweat it. They are hard to understand, but stick with it. We'll at least give you some pointers about pretending you get them.*

Week

one

Do it this way or do it your own way, just do it!

How to Read This Book This Week		
	Monday	read "Being a Guy Is Good"
	Tuesday morning	read "You Are Man Enough"
	Tuesday night	read "Believe in Yourself"
	Wednesday	Take The day off
	Thursday	read "ConTrol Your Mind"
	Friday	go on a DaTe NighT: CiTy Bus
	Saturday	day off
	Sunday	do your Focus Group

Being a guy is GOOD!!

or, no hitting, no spitting, no pow-pow.

by Justin Lookadoo

Girls. They're the sweetest thing on the planet, aren't they? They smell so good and feel so soft. Girls are amazing. And the spaz-o part is that they think the very same thing about us. Okay, they don't think we're soft or smell good, but despite our need to fart louder, spit farther, and burp bigger, girls still like us. Go figure. I know it's hard to believe, but I have it on good authority that it's true. What they like about us is that we are different from them. They might not know it, but that's what attracts them to us. In fact, it's an animal thing. They need us. Since the day the first caveman swatted at the giant pterodactyl, men have been the tough ones. We fight the wars, save the country, and rescue the beauties. It's God's plan, so we can't argue. We gotta break stuff, kill things, and get dirty. It's just part of the male nature.

The other day I heard a little girl reciting what she heard in day care: "No hitting, no spitting, no pow-pow" (no pow-pow meant no using your finger as a gun). In other words, the day care is run by sweet little women and is raising a bunch of sweet little women, even if they *are* little boys. Can you imagine little boys not getting to spit or hit or play with pretend weapons? They might as well say no farting, no blowing milk out your nose, and no mud fights. Why be a boy if you can't, well, be a boy?

16

My nephews and I have a different kind of relationship. I teach them all the stuff boys need to know. Essential stuff like how to spit, how to hit, and how to make a pretend gun out of anything. But I also teach them *when* they can do this and when they can't. It's like this: If they're going to hit me, they'd better hit me with all they got, because I'm coming after them, and I can hit a lot harder than they can. But along with that, they'd better not ever, ever hit their granny, or girls, or some kid at school just because he took the green crayon they like.

This is what God wants. He wants you to be every bit a male. But he wants it all to be under your control. That's everything. Anger, desire, sadness, sex—he wants you to have it all and for all of it to be under your control. Manly control.

HEAVY LIFTING
Where You Get Your Spiritual Workout

It's good that you are a guy. But any human with a penis is a guy. So let's get down to the real issue of being a man. To do that we have to start with the basics. We have to break it down all the way to the DNA and wiring. This is big-time important. You need to understand how we as males are unique and different from girls. So I want you to make a list. **Write down all the ways that guys are different from girls.** Yeah, there's **the physical stuff.** We're stronger, we're faster, we jump higher. But don't get stuck there. Write down **the emotional stuff** too. We are more emotionally stable. More fact oriented. It doesn't matter if it seems to be a good diff or a bad. Just write it down. List all the stuff that you can think of that makes us different from girls. Don't just skip ahead, do it!

17

How'd it go? Tough, wasn't it? You know why? Two reasons, and they're both male:

1. Guys don't think in emotional terms, so it's hard for us to make a list of emotional or spiritual differences that go beyond the obvious physical stuff.

2. You didn't know *why* you were doing this, and guys need a reason to get involved in something. They need to know the *why*. And "This is important" is not a good enough reason for most of us. So a lot of you had trouble because you didn't know the purpose.

So here's the answer to "Why are we doing this?": to understand girls.

Now look at the stuff you do have listed. You can tell that guys have their own male thing happening. The stuff that makes us unique is how God planned it. These are the things that God wants to use to change you from just another dude into a powerful warrior of God.

All the stuff you did here, focusing on what makes you a guy, was to let you know that these things are good. They are God. He's all about good. You are different from girls, and that's the way God wants it. No, that's the way he *needs* it.

Just to drive the point home, get out and spend the day checking out the differences between guys and girls. People-watch and see if you can get your list of guy gear even longer.

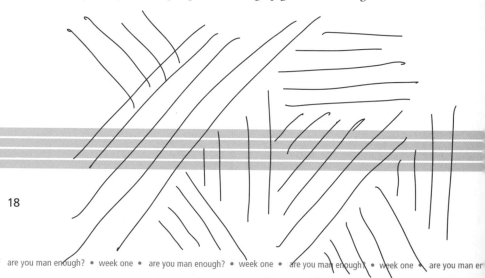

18

You are Man Enough

by Justin Lookadoo

Every little boy is born with a question in him that must be answered: **"Am I man enough?"** He starts searching for the answer as soon as he can play. In every fairy-tale fantasy **he is the hero, slaying the dragon, rescuing the beauty.**

Remember the stick? You had to have one. **A single stick could become all kinds of powerful things.** It was a **sword** to kill the monster. It was a **rocket launcher** to blow up the enemy. It was a **bat** to hit the winning home run. All in the quest to find out, "*Now* am I man enough?"

As a boy grows up, he starts looking at the world around him to find out how he will know when he is a man. And if you look around, it's easy to find out what the world says it takes to be a real man. **The Big 3.** Sex, money, power. Movies, music, and even video games teach every boy that if you want to be a man, you have to have the Big 3. Especially the honeys. Bodacious broads are crucial to the MTV male and the *007* action hero. You have to be a stud. Hooking up with the hotties makes you a real man. If hot chicks dig you, then the world says, "Yes, you *are* man enough."

But here's the **flaw in that logic:** If sexing the girls makes you a man, then after you've done it, the nagging question "Am I man enough?" should be answered, and you could quit chasing chicas. That's not what happens, though. The more sex a guy has, the more the question shouts, **"Am I man enough?"** which drives him searching for more. **The man question is**

19

never really answered by sex, money, or power. It only gets louder.

"So then how the heck *does* this question get answered?" you ask under your breath as if I can hear you. Thanks for asking. The answer is, it's a guy thing. Hang with me now and I'll try to explain it using this simple biblical example in less than 14 seconds—go!

When Isaac was old and almost blind, he called for Esau, his older son, and said, "My son?" "Yes, Father?" Esau replied. "I am an old man now," Isaac said, "and I expect every day to be my last. Take your bow and a quiver full of arrows out into the open country, and hunt some wild game for me. Prepare it just the way I like it so it's savory and good, and bring it here for me to eat. Then I will pronounce the blessing *(that you are man enough)* that belongs to you, my firstborn son, before I die."

Genesis 27:1–4 (words in italics added by author) (by author I mean me) (by me I mean Justin)

Did you catch it? It was a fastball. But check it out: Isaac was the only one who could tell Esau that he was man enough. His job as father was to tell his son he was now a man. Throughout history it's been men who pass on manhood to boys. **"Am I man enough?" can only be answered by another man.** Not a woman. Not a mom, a grandmother, not all the girls you can sleep with. The answer can only be passed down from man to man. That's how God set it up. This isn't just a human thing either. It's an animal kingdom thing too. If left to themselves in the wild, young male animals would destroy the world around them more than you could believe.

Cut to short detour pertaining to animal behavioral sciences: On a game reserve in Africa, a group of **boy elephants** (technical term for male of the species) was brought in from an over-crowded section of the country (or "bussed," as we refer to it in the inner city). The rangers, being people and not elephants, thought these tykes were old enough to figure out how to be big elephants on their own. Unfortunately, it didn't work out that way. Elephants usually stay away from humans and stick to themselves. But things changed when this group of young guy elephants was moved in and allowed to roam the jungles unsupervised. Soon their elephant testosterone was raging and they were banging their heads together like 'roid-raged football players who just scored a touchdown. And they didn't stop with each other. They turned into a vicious gang of marauding juvenile delinquents. And in a 5-year period, **these little elephant thugs killed more than 40 white rhinos, 2 tourists, and a bunch of cars.**

As a last-ditch effort to get these hooligans under control, the directors (the humans, that is), decided to call in reinforcements. And who better to wup-up on some *little* male elephants than *big* male elephants? So 6 full-grown males were airlifted into the park. Suddenly these boy elephants weren't the big guys on campus. The attacks stopped. Their aggression subsided, and whadd'ya know if they didn't start acting like elephants instead of crazed lunatics. The old male elephants put their big, fat, stubby feet down and passed on their knowledge of how to be an adult male, and the love between man and elephant was restored.

Okay, I know this is going to be a stretch, but **can you think of any other society where large numbers of young males are left alone without involved, adult male role models?** A society where these young males have to figure out how to become adult males without anyone really showing them how? A place where boys are turning aggressive, fighting, and have no respect for rules, order, or authority? (If you haven't made the connection by now, then you probably aren't able to read this book, either, so we're not going to worry about you.)

That's right. **It's us.** We are the same as those elephants. The difference is that the elephants only had a few young males who had to figure out what to do on their own. We have millions of young males who are trying to figure out how to become men with no men to guide them. The only help we have is other young males who don't have a clue about being a man either or caring mothers and grandmothers who don't get it. Either way, it doesn't work. **It takes an adult male to answer the question "Am I man enough?" for a younger male.** That's the way it works in the animal kingdom, and that's the way it works in the people kingdom.

I know that most of you have never really thought about this before, but don't shut it out as bogus just because it's new. It's gonna start making more sense, I promise, or I'll give you your money back (except the part I've already spent . . . which is all of it, so don't ask).

Guys do what they do to get the manhood question answered. And remember, **it's a guy thing. Women cannot give manhood to boys.** When I was growing up my mom called me "Sweetheart." I loved the sound of that, but it didn't let me know I was a force to be reckoned with. **My dad called me "Man-man."** Now that was a name. Not only was I a man, but I was a man times 2. Mom was there to nurture me. Dad was there to let me know that I was a man.

I still remember when Dad got in big trouble over this. We had a horse that we were trying to break so we could ride it. We worked with it for a few weeks, but it just wouldn't let us do the riding thing. Dad and I woke up early one Saturday morning (before Mom got up), and Dad said, "Go out there and get on that horse." I walked out the back door, grabbed the saddle, and walked toward the arena. The whole time I was walking, I

22

was thinking, "I can't do this." But Dad had told me to, so I was going to do it. I saddled up the horse and put my foot in the stirrup. I swung my leg over, plopped in the saddle, and froze. Nothing happened. I was okay. I pried my tiny fingers from the death grip I had on the saddle, and the horse and I started our ride. About 30 minutes later my dad came out and said, "You're looking good. How does she feel?" I smiled with all the pride I had in my little body and said, "Great." He smiled back and said, "I knew you could do it."

Guess what? **That day I got a new swagger in my step.** My question, "Am I man enough?" was being answered in the real world by a real man.

What I didn't realize was that Dad was watching me from the window to make sure I was all right. Mom woke up and asked what he was doing. When he explained what was happening, she went ballistic on him and tried to rush out to the arena. Wouldn't it have done wonders for my ego if my mommy would have run out there and made me get off the horse so I wouldn't hurt myself? **Sometimes a man has to step up and do what a woman couldn't understand. Manhood is about risk and danger, and women just don't get that.**

I was lucky to have both a mom and a dad, because when a boy doesn't have a man to guide him, he usually ends up going in one of two directions. He goes out searching like the young elephants—turning to violence, aggression, drinking, partying, sex, anything and everything that seems to be wild and dangerous. Or he totally quits. He becomes passive and polite, never taking a risk, what some might call a "momma's boy." What happens is that if he isn't finding out that he is man enough, he snaps into his feminine side. It's not a gay thing—we all have masculine and feminine sides. But this guy goes into that mode and never snaps out of it. He stays safe, comfortable, risk-free.

23

No one has ever pushed this guy to be wild, to feel his own strength, to be a man.

That is why I'm here. **I want you to see your strength.** I want you to feel the **manly blood pumping** life into your soul. Listen, I am telling you this from one man to another. **You *are* man enough. You *are* powerful.** You *are* a man to be reckoned with. You have all the strength, passion, power, and umph to be a real man.

HEAVY LIFTING

So here's the deal. I spent a few pages pounding one thing into your thick head. And that thing is that **manhood can only be passed down from a what?** Yes, from another dude, from another man.

You know they say knowledge is power. Well, that's donkey doo. Knowledge is powerless if you don't *do* anything with it. So here's what you're gonna do. First, think. I know it's hard, but try. Who do you have in your life that is passing manhood on to you? If it's your dad, awesome. But just because your dad is still with you doesn't mean he is passing manhood on to you. Who is telling you that you are man enough? A teacher? A neighbor? Youth pastor? Mentor? Who? Think of one man. Then think of one situation where he has helped show *you* how to be a man.

If you can't think of someone, it's time to take control of your maleness. Think of all the possible male donors in your life and make a list. Then get to work. Find out which one of these men would like to pass his manhood truths on to you. One of the hardest things I ever did was ask my current mentor to help me. But I finally had to suck it up and take him to lunch, and it went something like this:

24

Me: "I need somebody to help me. I need somebody who has been where I want to go, and it's you. If you are willing to mentor me and help me, that's awesome. If not, that's cool too. It's not a big deal one way or the other." (It was a big deal to me, but I was trying to play it cool.)

He looked at me and smiled. (I mean, think about it. Who wouldn't want to hear from a younger guy that he wants his life to be like yours?)

Him: "I can't say no. Let's do it."

It was that easy. Still scary, but easy.

So get to list-makin'. Here's your chance to make your manhood happen. Don't miss it. It's about the rest of your life.

If you're having a tough time getting why you need a mentor, think about this stuff. God wants you to listen up. Get your Bible out and look up this stuff:

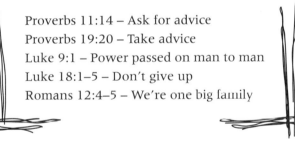

Proverbs 11:14 – Ask for advice
Proverbs 19:20 – Take advice
Luke 9:1 – Power passed on man to man
Luke 18:1–5 – Don't give up
Romans 12:4–5 – We're one big family

Believe in YOURSELF

by Justin Lookadoo

So where are we? First you figured out that your guy stuff is exactly how God made you totally different from girls. Then it was all about getting that mentor. Now it's about sabotage. Here's the story, the Fairy Tale Gone Bad:

Once upon a time, a boy was born a powerful warrior. Dangerous. Tough. Always looking for the next adventure. No one had to tell him to take risks; he just did it. **But one day he got knocked down.** His confidence was shattered. People did and said things to crush his image and which made him believe he was no longer good enough and that he was slow, weak, and just flat-out unlikable. The little boy's shot at manhood was smeared out, struck down, waylaid. And ever since then he's asked the question, "Am I man enough?"

Every guy has at least one of those moments, that first time when he realized that he wasn't man enough. **Think back.** Can you remember the first time you felt weak? It might have been something your dad said or did. It might have been something another guy said when he was making fun of you. What's the first time you remember? If you don't know when the first time was, just think of *a* time, any time when your ego took a blow and you felt like a complete dork.

See, it's **a great plan of God's enemy to convince God's powerful creation (that's you) that he (that's you again) isn't powerful at all.** Then the enemy can play on a guy's

26

natural instinct and inborn need to be powerful by convincing him that he isn't powerful by himself. After that's accomplished, he can get him to do some really stupid stuff to prove to himself that he *is* man enough. But you need to realize that if **you were really made in God's image, then you must have been made right**—no broken parts, nothing falling off, nothing too small, too soft, or too short. You were perfect at one time. When did it all go downhill? When did you buy the lie? When did being a man become defined as "anything but you"?

Think about it. **When was the first time you realized you weren't man enough?** When was the first time the pure you wasn't enough? Remember? It will probably be the first thing you think of, since your subconscious remembers it oh so well.

I know it's hard to think about this stuff—this is a new mental trip for a lot of guys—but try. Try to think of the first time you felt like the man in you was shoved down. You were hurt. Abused. Made fun of. Some of you will be able to think of something quickly. Even several things. But for some of you this will take a little longer. Stick with it until you find out. It could be something like:

- **Your dad walked out when you were young.** And you became the man of the house, but nothing you did seemed to make things any better. Your mom would talk about how horrible your dad was and then say those words that would destroy your soul: "You are just like your father."

- **Your dad was a perfectionist or overbearing.** You always wanted to do stuff with him, but every time you tried, he would tell you that you were doing it wrong. He would get all upset or tell you to hurry up because

27

you were too slow. Or maybe he just made fun of everything you did.

When you played ball you went to the locker room and took a shower like everyone else. And the **guys made fun of you** because you were too fat, too skinny, too hairy, or didn't have any hair yet. They totally made you feel like there was something wrong with you.

It could be almost anything. Keep thinking. Don't move on until you find a time when you felt like you weren't a man.

Got it? Okay, now I believe at that point in time **your fierce manhood began to be covered up.** Notice I didn't say "taken away," 'cuz it can't be, but it sure can be covered up so that you forget it's even there. That first time someone covered up your power with weakness, that moment in time when the little boy lost his warrior spirit, **that is your manhood's defining moment.** But that's okay, because **we are going to redefine it.** We are going to remix your thoughts as if it were a bad Kelly Osbourne song (just pick one). We are going to take away that moment and replace it with a new, more honest defining moment. See, whatever happened eons ago has no real bearing on who you really are and how much of a real man you become. You only think it does, or at least your subconscious thinks it does. See, **your brain is kinda like a dog.** It only believes what you tell it. That's why brainwashing works so well. Sit. Lie down. You are getting very sleepy. When people hear things over and over, they start to believe it, and sometimes it only takes one traumatic event to reprogram a lifetime of thought.

In the next few pages **you are going to take back your mind** and your manhood. Are you man enough? The answer is yes. You are man! And I am here to tell you that.

28

Heavy Lifting

Today look up these verses and start to let them ooze through your mind. This is going to get you squared. Write them down. This gets the words mainlining to your brain. If you're gonna play, play to win, and getting these verses in your head will set you up for a win.

Isaiah 54:17

Luke 17:6

2 Timothy 1:7

1 Peter 1:13

Now here's the vibe. After you write the verses, you can stop for the day, relax, and get ready for tomorrow. Or you can keep the momentum and power going through the next few pages. Either way we won't think less of you. (I mean, how could we?) You choose. Check you later, or right now, whatever.

When did being a man become defined as "anything but you"?

CONTROL YOUR MIND
by Justin Lookadoo

All right now, back in the saddle. Remember that first time you felt like you weren't man enough, that defining moment we harped on earlier? Time to take it on. Most guys have never dealt with the issues that crush their spirits. They happen and you believe whatever you heard. You believe that you are stupid, or weak, or just a loser. But listen, if you don't change these memories, then that will become your identity for the rest of your life. You will become weak and stupid, and you will lose your passion and fire for the cool stuff life is all about.

The thing about our brain is that we _can_ change our memories. We _can_ change how we remember things. We do this all the time automatically, but now we are going to do it on purpose. We are going to change the way we remember this totally negative self-history and turn it into something powerful, not a man-crushing event. Check out Romans 12:2 and **write it down here.**

This is what we are going to do today—reprogram (renew) your mind. So hold on to your gray matter, 'cuz here we go.

HEAVY LIFTING

Okay, go someplace you can be alone. Take your **Bible** and a **pencil (or the writing utensil of your choice).** Go to your

30

room, a basement, anywhere no one will bother you for **at least 20 minutes**. Make sure you are comfy and the room is quiet. Don't have the TV, music, or IM's going. It won't kill you to shut it down for a few ticks.

If this changing your thinking thing sounds a little too freaky, that's cool. But check it out, it's totally scriptural. **Write down Philippians 4:8 here:**

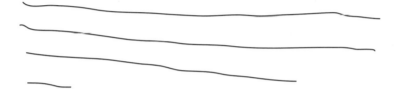

Again, I'm not telling you to write it down because I want you to work on your penmanship. It's so it will get stuck in your head quicker. So do it.

Look at it. What does it say? Whatever that major negative you have from the past is, it doesn't fit into the list of things to think about.

Just to make sure that it's coming through loud and clear, here's a little quiz. (Oh, quit whining, just take the quiz.)

Quiz: Philippians 4:8

1. I am supposed to control my thoughts.   T   F
2. I have the ability to become happy by thinking good stuff.   T   F
3. God wants me to think only true and good stuff.   T   F
4. It isn't what happens to me, but what I *think* about what happens to me that matters.   T   F

31

5. Bad memories make for bad feelings, and God isn't about bad.   T   F

6. God hates it when I lie to myself.   T   F

Scoring: *Give yourself one point for every True you circled and two points for every False you circled. Then add 'em up.*

5–6: Mr. Man! *Way to go. You're getting it. God wants you to be in control of your thoughts. 'Cuz if you aren't, then who the heck is?*

7–8: Mind over matter. *You are so close yet so far. You're almost there; you just need to start telling yourself the truth **all** of the time, not just when it's convenient.*

9–12: Dang, dude! *What's up with you? Do you think that someone else can take better control of your life than you can? Go back and check out these verses. Write 'em down. Memorize 'em. Meditate on 'em. Do whatever it takes to get your brain to kick into the fact that God wants you to get control of it. Here they are: Romans 12:2; James 3:2; 4:7; 2 Peter 2:19.*

Enough blabbin'; let's do something. I want you to **think about that time when you felt like you weren't good enough, tough enough, man enough.** Remember that event that destroyed your manhood, or rather covered it up. **Let the scene run in your mind** like I'm sure it has before. See the sights, hear the words. Feel the hurt, the pain, the insults. Feel everything that happened. Whether it was your dad, an uncle, your mom, a kid in the locker room, whoever and whatever, let it run through your mind.

Then here's what you are going to do. (Don't start yet; read first.) **Go back to the same sitch.** Start running it like you remember it. **Then I want you to see** something you've never seen: **Jesus standing there.** See him going through the whole thing with you. And with every accusation or horrible thing said

32

or done, look at him. Listen to him and hear what he has to say to you. While the bad stuff is happening, **hear him telling you the truth.** Hear him telling you that you are smart. **That you are strong.** That he made you exactly like you are because he needs you to be that way. You are perfect. Whatever the situation, whatever was done or said, see him changing it. Hear him telling you how much he loves you. See Jesus commanding his angels to go take up your slack and kick some bootay. I know it may be tough, but you can do it.

When you get to the end, you will run the whole thing over again and still see Jesus there with you telling you what he believes about you. "You are powerful. You are God's mighty warrior, made to fit his purpose in the war."

This changes the memory. When this negative stuff happened to you, Jesus was there trying to tell you the truth; you just didn't see him or hear him. He was there, and his angels were ticked off that someone was trying to crush the spirit of God's man. This time you get to see him—no, you *have* to see him. This is your first step in regaining your status as a warrior, a champion, a bold fighter for the King.

Before you shut your eyes to remember, I want you to get psyched. Get motivated by the holy Word and what it says about God. See, it's the Creator himself who is going back into your memory with you to change your life. Here are some verses to look up. Write them down right here. Either read them out loud or in your head shout them like a warrior. Even better, if you are alone, shout them out loud. Get amped! Christ is going to open a can of . . . uh, of beating up the hiney of the enemy. He will destroy the old memories and bring in the new. Now look 'em up and write 'em down!

Isaiah 54:17 – No one can whip you _____
Luke 17:6 – You can do anything _____

33

Hebrews 4:16 – Be bold _____

Matthew 28:18 – He has complete authority _____

John 16:33 – He kicked butt _____

2 Timothy 1:7 – You got the power _____

Okay, it's time to get started. **Shut your eyes, go through the memory,** and see Jesus there with you, just like we talked about up above. Hear what he's saying. You are clearing the way for you to become a powerful warrior for the one true God.

Do this 2 times right now. Don't move on until you've done it. Go.

Do this every day for a whole week. It will be a lot easier tomorrow and even easier the next day. Every time you do this, you are changing the way your mind sees what happened to you. You are renewing your mind. Dude, it's scriptural. You always wanted to know how to connect the Bible to your real life? Well, here ya go. Now do it 1 more time before you leave. Come on, just 1 more time, do it! This is where it's at. You learn to control your mind, then you can control your world. You will be the leader, not the follower. The head, not the tail. You will be a man in control of his future and his destiny.

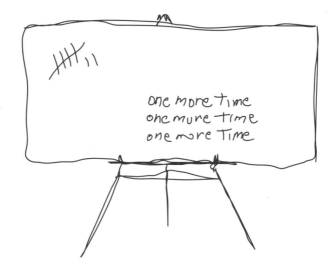

DATE NIGHT
CITY BUS

Date Night—it isn't what you think. It isn't about hooking up or making out; it's about a night to get together with your girlfriend or your group to do something different. It's not a sexual thing or even a romantic thing; **it's an adventure thing.** On Date Night you are going to **push your limits.** You are going to **think about things you've never thought about before** and **do things you've never done before.** You are going to **get out of the house** and maybe even out of the neighborhood. You are going to **find out things about yourself** and about your girlfriend or friends. So don't get the wrong idea, your Date Night is going to be **a dare night.** Dare yourself to get out of your comfort zone and get involved in the circle of life (sorry, bad *Lion King* reference).

Okay, here's the plan for your first Date Night. Do this on whatever night of the week you want to. If you're following the "How to Read This Book" steps, you'll do it on Friday, but hey, you're big kids now, so you can do it whenever you want to. Your choice, but our rules.

City Bus

The city bus. You've seen it. You've heard it. And you've most definitely smelled it. It's the blood vessel of the city, carrying all the workers to their jobs and all the shoppers to their stores. It's sometimes filthy, sometimes loud, and sometimes lonely. The people who ride it don't seem to have a lot of energy. They aren't all smiles, and they definitely aren't social. Until today.

Your mission, should you choose to accept it, is to buy a ticket for the city bus. Don't know how? Good, that's part of

35

the adventure. Figure it out. Buy your ticket and board the bus. **You have one goal: to make people feel like someone cares about them.** Many of the people you will find on the bus will be empty inside. And lots will be angry. So don't play the freak. Don't cross into their personal space, push yourself on them, or try to make them hug you. But do try to **do stuff that you think might make a stranger's day.** Pay the fare for the working woman who is getting on in a hurry. Carry the bags for the old lady you see standing on the street corner waiting to get on. Tell the girl sitting next to you that you like her coat. Make small talk that makes people feel good.

You are Christ's hand on their lives. If you want to pray for them, try this. Sit in the back of the bus and **imagine Jesus getting on the bus.** Imagine him walking down the aisle and sitting by someone. What would he say to them? Imagine it. How would he interact with people? Imagine it. This is your prayer, your imagined prayer. God knows your thoughts before they are words, so this is your way of asking his blessing on the lives of people. Get to know the outgoing ones. Offer to help the weak ones. Enjoy life! Enjoy God's creation. And enjoy one another.

Explore life. Explore your night. And most of all, have a wonderific time.

Location Note: If there aren't any bus routes near you, drive over to the nearest big city. And if that's just too dang far, then figure out some other way to do things like this for people. Meet people at Wal-Mart, pump gas, or go to a busy neighborhood. Be creative.

Stupidity Prevention Notice: Now don't be a fool and go into some dangerous neighborhood you've never been to before, and if you're 14, don't just go jump on a bus and get your parents all freaked out. You and your girlfriend or your group should do

36

this together. If your group is big, split up into groups of 4. Be safe. Be smart. Talk it over with your fam, your youth pastor, whoever. Let someone know where you're going. But be daring and try a new route, one you've never taken.

Road Trip Wrap up

When you are done, get back together and chat about your night:

What happened?
How did it feel?
Who did you meet?
Why did you do what you did?
What did Jesus think of it all?
Was your prayer effective?

Focus Group

1. He Said, She Said Improv—guys play girls and girls play guys
2. Show-and-Tell – what did you do, learn, see all week?
3. Q&A – each side asks 5 questions

1. Group ACTIVITY—He said, She said IMPROV

If you are doing this book in a group, get ready for a switcheroo. This week you get to show the girls what you really think of them by playing them. Check it out. (If you are doing this with just your crush, then you can skip to the next section, Show-and-Tell, unless you feel really artistic and just want to do your own improv.)

Sick of the stupid things girls say and do? Now's the time to show 'em. Today you get to be a girl. No, you don't have to wear their bras and panties, so just relax. It's just 20 minutes of emotional cross-dressing. Then you can go play some ball to restore your masculinity. We've listed three scenarios here. You'll need thespian volunteers, 4 girls and 4 guys. In these sketches the girls act out the guys' part and the guys are the girls. You can use props, hats, wigs, dresses, whatever. Each improv should be 3 to 5 minutes long with 2 to 4 people involved. Have fun!

> **The Big Date** (2 girls, 2 guys) – The guy (played by the girl) has to pick up the girl (played by the guy) for a date. Meet the parents. Drive to the restaurant. Order dinner, eat, and then go home.

> **The Crush** (2 guys, 2 girls) – In 2 groups of friends, the girls and the guys like each other but are afraid to say so. They go out together. How do they all act around each other? (Remember, girls play the guys and guys play the girls.)

38

The Breakup (1 or 2 guys, 1 or 2 girls) – The guy (played by the girl) wants to break up with the girl (played by the guy). How will he do it? How will she react? Friends can be involved if you want.

Note: These are just ideas to get you started. You can change 'em up however you want. You are the *artiste* (say this in French, it sounds better).

2. Show-and-tell

We'll get to the Q&A soon, but before you start the interrogations, give each other a leg up and tell the girls what your week was about. Give them the highlights of what you learned, did, and experienced. They did different stuff than you, so fill 'em in so you are all on equal ground. Take 5 minutes to show and tell.

3. Q + A

Okay, now you can start the games! This is the same drill as the kickoff: **5 questions for the girls, 5 questions for the guys, 5 minutes to answer each one.** Ask away. Here are some discussion questions to get you started, or you can make them up on your own. Asking this kind of guy Qs will help you get to the bottom of the female psyche. But careful, don't get lost in there!

- What do you want us to do when we like you?
- Why do girls say stuff like "I'm too fat" and "I'm not pretty"?
- Why do girls fight with each other?
- Why do you go to the bathroom in packs?

39

Dateabk guys Love

ADVENTURE

You can read it like this or go it alone.
Read it however you want to this week.

How to Read This Book This Week		
	Monday	read "Don'T JusT WanT a Win, WanT an AdvenTure"
	Tuesday	read "Men of God Are Wild, NoT DomesTicaTed Animals"
	Wednesday	read "Tace Your Fears"
	Thursday	read "Read God inTo IT"
	Friday	DaTe NighT: The Wild Side
	Saturday	Take The day off
	Sunday	Focus Group

DON'T JUST WANT A WIN, WANT AN ADVENTURE

by Justin Lookadoo

How's the whole renewing the mind thing going? Have you been doing it? If you have, man, I'm proud of you. Even if I haven't met you yet, I'm sending out the "I'm proud of you" vibe. You are truly going to become a powerful warrior of God.

If you haven't done it, stop now. Go back and do the renewing your mind stuff before you start today. Can't remember what I'm talking about? Go back and read "Controlling Your Mind" again. I ain't yo momma. If you haven't done it and refuse to, don't come crying to the rest of us fellas when we're conquering the world and you're still stuck in wussdom. For the rest of us, let's get our smash on!

Okay, now that you have your mind-renewing power pack turned on and running smoothly, let's take a look at this whole adventure thing. The quest to answer the question, "Am I man enough?" leads us right **into the face of adventure.** We have to have it. We do whatever it takes to make life exciting.

And the great thing about it is that **God is all about adventure.** He's the one who made us to crave it, and he sets us up so we can live bigger adventures than we could ever dream of.

Now let's make sure we are talking about the same stuff here. When you hear the word *adventure,* what pops into your mind? Write it down. Quick. The first 2 things you think of when I say *adventure:*

42

Take an eye at your list and then check this. Here is the actual definition of *adventure:*

> 1. an undertaking of uncertain outcome
> 2. a hazardous enterprise

Compare that to the list you made. Is that what you were thinking of when you thought of adventure? Not me. I was thinking of fun, excitement, a rush. Not "an undertaking of uncertain outcome."

Play movie critic here. Think about **an adventure movie** you have seen. Yeah, sitting there in your seat, it was over-the-top cool. It was what you wanted. The adventure. The excitement. But think about the movie. **Put yourself *in* the movie.** No, not in a script written for you to come out the hero, but in the actual situation the hero is in. Now think—where's the fun?

There you are **walking down the street,** minding your own business, when a van rolls up beside you. **Two guys jump out and slam you into the van.** They spend the next three days beating the pigeon poo out of you. They are asking you all these questions about what you know, and you don't have a clue what they are talking about. You have no food, no water. They throw you into a cell with no toilet, no clothes. You curl up in a ball in the corner with **blood running down your mouth,** not knowing what they are going to do to you next. **Where's the fun in that?** Adventure has nothing to do with fun. Adventure is "an undertaking of uncertain outcome."

So when our Creator put the desire for adventure in our hearts, **it was not an "if it feels good, do it" kind of thing.** And even more important to understand, it's not an external, physical thing that "happens" to you. See, **the adventure that is written on your soul is a spiritual adventure.** We are all spiritual beings. And so we have the need to be engaged in **a spiritual adventure—a spiritual undertaking of uncertain outcome.**

43

Do you agree that God wants you to have adventure? Just nod your head. Listen, God put that desire in you. It has to be fulfilled. And if you still don't believe me, look how he proves his love for adventure over and over.

Check out Gideon. Here's the run-down. He was just an **average guy.** Well, if you asked him he was below average. He was from **the weakest clan.** (Back in Bible days, clan meant all your fam. The cousins, uncles, nephews, the whole clan.) He was working with his wheat down inside a huge winepress so the enemy couldn't see him. He was weak and scared. This guy needed an adventure to revive his soul.

Well, while Gideon was working/hiding, this dude came and started talking to him. It was really an angel, but Gideon didn't know that right off. This guy told Gideon that God had chosen him to save Israel, and instantly Gideon spewed out all the reasons why he *couldn't* possibly do it. **He was ordinary, scared,** puny—in fact his whole family was quite well known for being puny.

Finally, Gideon figured out that he had been talking to an angel, and he was blown away.

> Then the angel of the LORD touched the meat and bread with the staff in his hand, and fire flamed up from the rock and consumed all he had brought. And the angel of the LORD disappeared. When Gideon realized that it was the angel of the LORD, he cried out, "Sovereign LORD, I have seen the angel of the LORD face to face!"
>
> Judges 6:21–22 NLT

After some heavy-duty praying and a few confirmations from God, Gideon said okay, he would do whatever God wanted.

If I were you, at this point I would go **read Judges 6–7** to get the full-screen view of what happened. If you're a slacker, jump in at Judges 7. Here's where the real adventure takes place.

See, Gideon got his massive army ready to win the battle. But remember, **God doesn't want a win, he wants adventure.**

Remember the definiton of adventure? If you have to look back, that's cool, but you should be pretty close to knowing it by now.

With that in your head, read Judges 7:1–22. Now look for the adventure.

Time passing. . . . Me waiting. . . . You reading. . . .

Did you see it? God not only wants adventure but he wants major adventure. **He wants a huge undertaking of uncertain outcome.** Did you catch that? Gideon had all these men, and God was like, "No, I want you to have an even bigger adventure." So he sent people home, then God said, "Even bigger!" and more warriors went home. And to make things God-sized, Gideon ended up with only 300 men and, to top it all off, their weapons were trumpets and clay jars. Wow. Now we have adventure!

Your life might not seem so huge. You don't have an army around you. You don't even see angels. But I can tell you, the adventure is there if you'll just look for it.

Time to play this out in your day-to-day. So here's what you're going to do: Throughout the week look at stuff that happens in your life and **find the adventure in it**—the uncertain outcome. When you **find it, do it.** When you see something coming and you get that little feeling in your stomach 'cuz you don't know if you can do it or not, take the risk and live the adventure. Ride it like a wave. No fear. No regrets.

Wuss-out disclaimer: This will be hard. Most of us have never been taught to seek out adventure. It's okay if you don't know what you're doing. It's just important that you try it. It won't go perfect, and that's great. Don't worry about what other people think. God just wants you to jump in.

45

Xtra credit

➤ **If you want to add even more spice** to your study, try this. Take **an adventure inventory.** Think about the past year, or your whole life if you want, and write down the adventures you've had. Remember, they're just undertakings of uncertain outcome. It could be giving a speech in front of class. It could be skiing for the first time. Telling someone you love them for the first time. You didn't know the outcome of something, and it might have been awful, but you did it anyway.

The last time I was in Colorado, a group of us went hiking through the mountains. We crossed rushing streams and jumped over obstacles. It was tons of fun, but that wasn't the adventure. The adventure came when I decided to climb up beyond the tree line and over thousands of boulders that had slid down the mountain earlier that year. Each rock was an avalanche waiting to happen. But I had to see how high I could go. Halfway up, the rocks started moving, so I had nowhere to go but up. One false move and I'd be rock bait. I must have gone up 1,500 feet when I stopped to look *down* on the mountaintops below me. My friends looked like ants snapping photos.

But wait, there's more. The biggest adventure was figuring out how to get down. It's always a lot easier going up. So I pretty much crawled all the way. Physically exhausted and emotionally charged, I ran down the rest of the mountain like a little boy on Christmas morning. Adventure is pure, high-octane fuel!

That was one of mine. Now it's your turn. Make a list. Find adventure in your spirit. Where was it? You don't have to write it all out like I did. You'd be cooler if you did, but you can just make a list and go mental with it. Think about how it felt to be in the adventure. And remember, it's not about the win—God wants you to experience the adventure.

Men of God Are Wild, not Domesticated Animals

BY JUSTIN LOOKADOO

Well-trained domesticated animals are nice. They go to the bathroom in the right place. They sit quietly by the table for scraps of food. They lie down when they are told to lie down, and they speak when they are told to speak. Great! **Obedient! Docile!** Domesticated animals. Every household needs one.

Now I don't want to step on any paws here, but some of you might actually *be* domesticated animals. You do what you are told. Obedient. Docile. **Afraid to risk** too much or try something where failure is an option. Now I'm not downing you if that is where you are right now. Many guys have been taught that risk is foolish, but I want you to know that God has other plans for you.

God loves the wild. He made you to be wild. That doesn't mean standing on your desk in the middle of class shouting like a hyena on crack. It means getting way out of your little comfort zone and taking a risk. **Wild animals stalk adventure.** They are made for the battle. So are you. If a wild animal stays in its comfortable little cave, it will die. It will never snag the food it needs. It will never mate. It will never live life. And the same goes for you. Risk is the only path that leads to spiritual adventure.

Risk = the possibility of loss or injury (loss of reputation or status or injury to emotions, ego, or pride, as well as physical loss or injury)

47

Check in with Bible guys. They had to risk tons and face their fears. Do you ever think of David as one who risked it all? If not, then you haven't checked out his life. He was the ultimate risk taker. Kind of **an extreme risk taker.** One story (1 Samuel 21:10–15) goes that after he ran away from the lunatic Saul, who wanted to kill him, he decided that the safest place to hide would be with the enemy. Duh! Who would look for you hiding out at your archenemy's house? And on that day it was the best option David could figure, so he headed for the camp of the Philistines and walked right in asking for the king, thinking he'd find asylum from Saul. Of course, that risk didn't pay off. They weren't too hip to the fact that the toughest guy on the other team had walked right into the king's tent. So get this, he had to act crazy to get them to throw him out. Nice recovery, David.

But later, when he had an army, he went back to that same king and risked hiding with the enemy again, and this time the risk paid off. They even gave him some of their best land to live on (1 Sam 27:2–7). Who would've thought? The biggest risk paid out the biggest reward, land and a home for his people. Risk—it makes kings and builds adventures.

The Bible is packed with this kind of stuff, and this is the stuff men are made for. Dive in and find out more about risk.

David goes to the Philistines: 1 Samuel 21:10–14

David goes back again: 1 Samuel 27

Moses takes Israel out of Pharaoh's hands: Exodus 12

Joseph plays interpret-the-dream-or-die: Genesis 41

Peter walks on water: Matthew 14:25-31

Philip talks to the African: Acts 8:29–38

This should get you excited and a little scared. This is what God has called his men (that's you) to be.

That's it for today. I just want you to keep thinking about these guys. About what they did and the risks they took. Ask yourself over and over and over today, **"Am I ready for the risk?"**

Hey, even write it down so that you will see it. In your locker, notebook, car, wherever it will catch your ojos (that's "eyes" in Española). And ask yourself, "Am I ready for the risk?"

FACE YOUR FEARS

by Justin Lookadoo

Risk + Adventure = Your life to the fullest

Okay, just like in 3rd grade, it's time for a review of the material. You got the definition of adventure. Ink it right here:

Now scribe the real meaning of risk:

So here's the $1.13 question (that's all the cash I have): What does this look like in the real world? Boil all the extra-fluffy feel-good out of the potion, and the common denominator is *fear*. So pull up your big boy pants, 'cuz it's time to jump into the deep end.

Here's the confusion. **We divide our life into two adventures: the physical adventure and the spiritual adventure.** The physical's easy. Jumping out of airplanes, snowboarding, skating on rails, whatever your adrenaline of choice is, physical adventure is obvious. But what the heck is spiritual adventure? Do they have a store for that kind of thing, like Heavenly Sporting Goods or Godly Goodies? Where do you go to get the equipment and the know-how to have a spiritual adventure?

Well, let's start with some of the basics of existence. Humans are made of spirit and body. Agreed? If you had just a spirit, you

50

wouldn't be human; you'd be a ghost or an angel or something. If you had only a body, you still wouldn't be human, 'cuz humans are made with a spirit. It takes both to make you a real human being. And since it takes both to be complete, you have to take care of both. One compliments the other. Keep this thought going for a sec. If we are both physical and spiritual, then we have to connect the dots that there is a spiritual adventure tied into every physical adventure.

First we gotta get to the core of what spiritual adventure is. Is it sitting in church and having a great worship time? Could be. Is it an amazing prayer time at your pad? Maybe. But for us, we are going to **consider a different kind of spiritual adventure.** One in the true sense of the word, **"an undertaking of uncertain outcome." A danger.** In this kind of real spiritual adventure, you don't know if you're going to make it or not. You don't know if the fear you feel in the bottom of your gut will kill you or take you to another level of existence. **A spiritual adventure is a battle.** It's like this: **You have a spiritual battle, or adventure, every time you cross out of your comfort zone into the uncomfort zone. It's when you risk.** When you do something that freaks the chicken doo out of you. Or that makes your gut ache and your pulse rage. It's pushing your mental and emotional limits.

Look at it like this. **A friend of mine is scared to death of flying.** It totally freaks him out and makes him nauseous, panicky, and just plain scared. So you'd think that he'd just avoid it, like most people. I mean, skip the tough stuff, life's too short, right? Wrong! If you want to be a real man with real adventure, then you say "no" to fear. His motto is, **"I won't be controlled by my fears."** So when fear comes, he stands right in its face and says, "Take your best shot." **He's a warrior.** But check this: A warrior isn't someone who has no fear; he's someone who has

51

fear but does the thing that scares him anyway. My friend travels all over the world. Risk + Adventure = Your life to the fullest.

And facing your fear is a **spiritual adventure. It's hand-to-hand combat with the enemy.** It's like saying, "You bring the fear and I'll bring the God, and let's see who wins."

See, a spiritual adventure is an internal adventure. It's the battle or the struggle you go through when you decide to fight off the lies of the enemy or the sins of your bod. If you have a hard time expressing your feelings to the people you love, then a spiritual adventure for you would be telling your best friend or even your brother that you love him. Or giving your mom flowers. If you're too embarrassed to protect the nerdy kid at school, then your spiritual adventure would be to step up and protect him. Stand in the face of your fear and insecurities.

In this kind of "spiritual adventure-seeking," a funny thing is going to happen. You are going to discover your man-heart. And **you are going to discover God's heart.** Every time you step up to the challenge, you will see that it won't kill you, and it will power slam you into the next risk, the next adventure.

So now it's up to you to decide. **Are the risks in your life worth the spiritual pay-off?** Are you ready to free-fall into the fire and rip off your pride, your fear, your insecurities to reveal the man inside? Or will you sit on the bench and wait 'til the time is right? You could be waiting forever.

HEAVY LIFTING

Check out these verses on power, strength, risk, and fear. **Pick 3 of them that you like and write each of them on a 3 x 5 card** or something else you can carry around with you. Then take those with you wherever you go this week. Look at 'em a lot, enough to memorize 'em. These are your weapons of war. Once your brain figures out that you have power, you will start to act more and more like a powerful man of adventure.

52

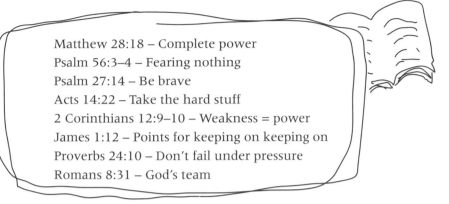

Matthew 28:18 – Complete power
Psalm 56:3–4 – Fearing nothing
Psalm 27:14 – Be brave
Acts 14:22 – Take the hard stuff
2 Corinthians 12:9–10 – Weakness = power
James 1:12 – Points for keeping on keeping on
Proverbs 24:10 – Don't fail under pressure
Romans 8:31 – God's team

All right, you're all amped up, so now what? Ink some more notes. What are some risks and adventures that you could get into this week? It could be standing up to everyone in the locker room when they're picking on the little nerdy kid. It could be helping an old lady carry her groceries out to the car. It could be starting a group at school to just walk around and pray through the halls like you did on the city bus Date Night. Remember, it's about risk, it's about adventure.

Find out your risks and go after them. Don't "wait for the opportunity to arise," make the opportunity happen. It's up to you. You're in or you're out. You're ready for risk and adventure or you're just going to stay in your fuzzy-slipper comfy-zone. Are you ready to become the man, the warrior God called you to be? Get going!

A message from your traitor: Yes, I, Justin, am a traitor. I'm not letting the fellas off the hook here. I am going to have the girls ask you about this in the focus group. I know, it's not nice to put you on the spot like that. And I really feel bad. . . . Oops, no, it was gas. I don't feel bad. So be ready to answer, "What did you risk this week?"

53

Read God into it

by Justin Lookadoo

S o, did you do anything yet? Have you taken the risk? Lived the adventure? Okay, it's only been a few hours, so I'll chill, but I will give you some things to do, some ways to get your brain focused on the right dog.

I don't know about you, but I don't feel like much of a prophet. When people start talking about what God "said" to them or "told" them to do, I check out. I've never heard God's booming voice saying "Justin, this is exactly what I want you to do next." I mean, sure, I have a *hunch* that he wants me to choose one thing or another. I've had *feelings* that what I was thinking was wrong, or true, or stupid. But I wouldn't say that he "told me" to do something. I'm totally clueless about what that means. So I've figured out a way of understanding him without the pressure of "Did I *really* hear him right?"

When I do something like ski down a humongous mountain or even watch a sunset, I say to myself, **"If God could speak to me through this, what would he say**?" And as soon as I do, my mind starts racing. I look at a **soda can** lying on the street and think of God saying, "Don't just get what you want out of me and then walk away. **Recycle.** Keep me in your life, even after you've gotten what you want." A student at one of my conferences told me he once saw a freaky-looking, tattoo-plastered, goth guy walking down the street in front of him and thought, *What would God say to me through this guy?* And suddenly he thought of God saying, "I died for him." And as he looked around, he thought the same thing about all the people on the street. "I died for him, and him, and her, and them." The kid had to stop for a sec just to take it all in. It's a trip. Give it a shot.

54

Next time you want to hear God's thoughts, ask yourself, "What could God be saying to me through this?"

Every day can be a spiritual adventure if you are willing to risk the unknown and think about what God might be saying.

Exodus 20:20—check it out. Write it here:

Today's the day you either pass the test or fail. Time to step up and know that you are man enough. Keep asking yourself, If God could speak to me through this, what would he say? The reason this works is because it takes the pressure off. You don't have to figure out if you really heard something or not.

This head trip threw my life into a spiritual adventure—a spiritual undertaking of uncertain outcome. And yeah, I have to keep reminding myself to do this. Many times a day I have those "Oh, I forgot" moments and have to get myself refocused on the question, "What could God say to me through this?"

Now let's check the physical side. Inside every physical adventure is the making of a great spiritual adventure. Risk, that getting out of your comfort zone, all kinda happens automatically in the middle of physical adventure. But how do you make the transition from the physical to the spiritual? How do you find God in the stuff you do? Is he there? What would he say if he were? Heck, what would you say back?

Here are some things to think on when you're ready for your next big physical adventure. If you're going to scale a major cliff, hang from a bungee cord, or snowboard down a black diamond, figure out how you'll see and hear God there. It works a lot better if you focus on this stuff before the big adventure.

- Find a trace of God in what you're doing.
- Listen to what he would say in it.

55

- See him in the amazing stuff all around you.
- Focus on the sounds around you. What are they saying?
- Trust God with your fears and insecurities.
- Lean into the pain, the fear, the unknown.

If you have a blonde moment and forget this stuff while you're in the middle of the fun, then just sit down afterward, alone or with your buds, and figure out what you remember about the adventure. What could God have said in it? What do you remember hearing and feeling? Stuff like that.

Accept your Manhood

All right, those are just a couple of ways to really headfirst swan dive into adventure. But before you actually set out on your life adventure, I want to talk straight with you. Listen to me very carefully. You are man enough! You can do this. You must! There is no other option. You are fierce. You are powerful. You are able to live the adventure. I don't care what has happened to make you believe otherwise. Some of us have been caught on the ropes, and every time we seem to get back on track, something else is said that catches us with a massive blow, and we just get beat down again. But listen, whatever has happened is a lie. Let it go. Don't let your past destroy your future.

Your dad thinks you're too sensitive, so he is emotionally pounding you to toughen you up. Or your mom is the only one around. She's doing her best, but you don't have anyone to show you how to be a man. You're too soft. Too weak. You're too small, your ears are too big, and you're not a powerful warrior. **All lies.** God made you. He put all this stuff in you—passion, confidence, adventure, power, desire to conquer and overcome challenge, it's all in you. You may never have had anyone show you how to use it or even tell you that it's in there, but it is. That's

56

who you are. Not because of what you're doing right now, but simply because that's how God made you. God doesn't see the weakness you see; he sees the man he made you to be. *What!*

What happens when I tell you that you are *not* man enough? You're not a warrior, you're not strong, you're not fierce. You're just a really polite guy. Better yet, what happens inside you when that girl you can't live without tells you, "You're just really a nice guy." If you're like most guys, a twitch of pain and defiance moves deep within you. You don't want to be *just* a "nice guy." When was the last time you heard a girl say, "Oh, I want him so bad—he is such a *nice guy*"? Nope. Nice is good, but not when it's *all* you have to offer. Okay, so use that defiance. Get motivated. Get mad. Get whatever ya have to get to get moving. You are more than just nice. You are a powerful warrior of the King.

When those thoughts of weakness and fear come and try to beat your spirit down, when you get a brief sane moment, say out loud "No!" Take a break and remind yourself of the way God sees you. The way he made you. A powerful warrior.

HEAVY Lifting

Earlier we talked about reprogramming your mind by renewing it with a cleaner and more masculine memory. Well, if you're still up for that psycho-babble kinda stuff, then check this out. A lot of your negative attitudes have to do with habit. Not just habits as in things you do a lot, but habits as in things you *think* a lot. Proverbs 23:7 says, "for as he thinks within himself, so he is" (NASB). Look at it like this: You are what you think. That means you can make yourself into what you want to become by controlling what you think. And you can see God more by making a habit of reading him into what you're doing. Are we making sense yet?

Okay, maybe this bit of heavy lifting will clear things up. Let's say you have a bunch of negativo thoughts about yourself. You aren't

57

man enough, you are a wimp, you can't be tough, stuff like that. Well, that's all the thoughts that run around in your head all day long. And your body, like a nice obedient dog, complies and makes sure to prove you right. And voilà, you become what you think you are. So to fix that, here's another little mind trick. Try this. Write down what you want to be. What you are. What you *will* do. Make it the best you that you can be. It goes something like this:

Learn

I am a man after God's own heart. I am strong and masculine. I will be tough and manly. I will protect girls and be a gentleman. I will defend the weak and stick up for the poor. I will be an honorable man, and I will be a wild man. I will risk everything for God. My pride, my ego, my heart—I will risk it all. I have a brave man living inside of me, and I am unleashing him today.

Psycho Note: Don't lie to yourself. Notice how I said stuff **I will do** and the stuff I wanted, if I didn't already have it. No lying to yourself. Just the truth about what you want to become. Then after you have written down all the stuff you want to be, your job is to read it out loud every morning before you leave the house. I know this sounds like a bunch of cocken-dwaddle, but trust me, it isn't. It really works.

This one too

Finally, brothers, whatever is true, whatever is noble, whatever is right, whatever is pure, whatever is lovely, whatever is admirable—if anything is excellent or praiseworthy—think about such things.

Philippians 4:8 NIV

The best way to make this verse happen is to do just what I said—write out the true, good, and pure stuff and think about it. Every day! Do it and you will see God everywhere and become the man you want to become.

58

DATE NIGHT — The WILD SIDE

Okay, it's time for you to exercise your dudeness. It's Date Night, and as the man, or one of the men of the group, it's your job to plan the date. This week the girls will do nothing except, well, be girls. Your job as the guy in the deal is to take her out on the Wild Side. Not *that* Wild Side, you dork. Tonight you're taking the girls to the zoo. (Country Boy Note: If you don't have a zoo for miles, you know the drill. Get creative. A big park, a farm, a creek, wherever nature shows off.)

Your mission this Date Night is to teach the girl(s) about how to find God in everything. If you've forgotten, go back and read the last chapter again. Teach them what you learned, then check out God around you. How do the bears remind you of him? The cheetahs? The chimps? Make the rounds. Keep asking the girls and each other about nature and where God could be in it. Then, after you've worked up a good appetite, sit down for a nice picnic dinner. And surprise! You're the ones bringing the dinner. Not the chicas! So read on.

Packing the picnic

You've packed your bags, you've packed your books, you might even have packed a gun, but have you ever packed a picnic? Well, as my first-grade teacher always said, "There's a first time for everything." But don't get your knickers in a wad, it's easier than it sounds. Here's what you do. Get a big basket or cool bag to hold all your goodies (a big garbage bag is out!). Decide what you'd like to eat—you can prepare it or buy it. Then make or buy enough for everyone. Besides grub, here's what you are going to need:

59

• dateable guys love adventure • week two • dateable guys love adventure • week two • dateable guys love adventure • week tw blanket

silverware (plastic might be best)

plates (paper all the way)

napkins

condiments (ketchup, mustard, salt/pepper, whatever you need for your concoction)

garbage bag (for trash, not as luggage)

drinks (for added flare, bring sparkling cider)

plastic cups (they even make 'em like wine glasses—cool!)

ice

For Bonus Points include:

throw pillows for softer sitting (comfort maker)

boom box with classical or romantic music (mood maker)

flowers (point maker)

moist towelettes (clean maker)

Dinner Conversation : chick note from Hayley

Remember, girls love to talk. Let us communicate with you and we feel like we have bonded. But it can be hard to think about things to talk about. So if you have a girl or a group of girls who aren't very chatty (yeah, I know, it's a stretch, but play along with me here), it helps to have an arsenal of questions to ask her/them, to draw her/them out and make her/them feel like you really do care about her/them. Listening to her/them means you care.

God topic: First it would be cool to talk about God and how you saw him today in the zoo.

60

vo • dateable guys love adventure • week two • dateable guys love adventure • week two • dateable guys love adventure • week

- Why do you think God gave Adam animals before he made Eve?
- Do you think there will be animals in heaven?
- What was your favorite time with God today?
- Which part of the zoo made you think about God's characteristics the most?
- How is the Holy Spirit like a monkey? (Don't ask me, it's just something to talk about.)

Girl topic: Then make sure to ask her about herself.
- What's your favorite kind of animal and why?
- What was the first animal you ever had?
- Did you come to the zoo a lot as a kid?
- If you could be any animal, what would it be and why?
- If I were an animal, which one would I be and why?

Other topics: The key to good conversation is asking questions. That means you are interested in what she has to say. So when she talks and you hear something you've never thought of or never heard before, ask her more about it. Something like this:

She says: I went to the zoo a lot when I was a kid.

You say: Who would take you?

She says: My dad.

You say: Are you guys close?

And so the conversation grows. See how one statement leads to another question? You'll always have something to talk about if you listen and think about learning more about her. So have fun! Get to planning. Oh, and don't forget to call the girl/girls to ask her/them to the zoo!

61

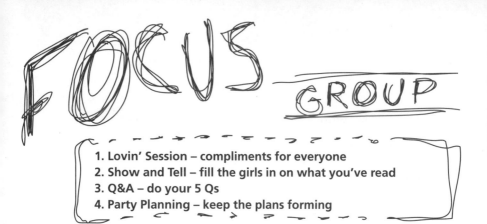

FOCUS GROUP

1. **Lovin' Session** – compliments for everyone
2. **Show and Tell** – fill the girls in on what you've read
3. **Q&A** – do your 5 Qs
4. **Party Planning** – keep the plans forming

So what did you learn this week? Anything? Did you get off your buttockomous and take a risk and a ride on the wild side? If so, most excellent. If not, I hope your group ridicules you in many languages. And now off to Focus Group wonderland. Yeah, you're going to do the normal focusing. You know, 5 questions for each group, discussion time, yadda yadda. But here's the added bonus. This time you are going to have a **Lovin' Session**.

For this you need to get your group into a big circle. Each person gets a blank piece of 8½ x 11 paper. Everyone has to write their name across the top of their paper and then pass it to the person to their right. That person is going to write a few sentences on your paper and then pass it on to the person on their right, and so on. These sentences will be compliments, things you like about the person whose name is on the paper. Share the love. "I love that you are so funny and cute. You make my day every time I see you. I am a better person because I know you." Stuff like that. This is a Lovin' Session! Build each other up. Encourage people in their gifts and let them know how much you care. At the end of the circle, you will get your own paper back and will be able to bask in the beauty of kind words for as long as you keep that paper. (**Girlfriend note:** If it's just you and your girlfriend, then you guys should take 5 minutes to write each other a nice note. Be generous with your words. It isn't every day that she gets to hear how great she is.)

62

After you have done your Lovin' Session, it's time to focus. Recap all that you've read for the girls so they know what's going on, and they will do the same for you. Then get to focusing. 5 questions for you and 5 for them. Same drill as before. Come up with your own questions.

Finish the night by working on the *Dateable* Bash—only one more week before blastoff. Will you be ready? Will the party be lame or legendary? It's up to you, so get the Bash on!

Week

3

You know the drill. Read it like this or **be a rebel** *and do it your own way.*

How to Read This Book This Week		
	Monday	read "Guys and Girls Need Each OTher"
	Tuesday	read "Be a GenTleman"
	Wednesday	Take The day off
	Thursday	read "The DaTe: Who Does WhaT?"
	Friday	DaTe NighT: Dinner and a Movie
	Saturday	Day off
	Sunday	Focus Group

Guys + Girls Need Each Other
by Hayley Morgan
—with interruptions by Justin

Competition. It's a good thing! It lets you know what you're made of. It lowers prices and raises adrenaline. It gives you power and pushes you to excellence—in just about every way but one. That one major place where competition kills is between a guy and a girl. Now don't get all huffy, big boy, I'm not talking about your precious ball game. I mean, if you're gonna play, play to win. But when guys and girls start competing with their roles in a relationship, things get messed up. If this isn't making much sense yet, good. I've got you right where I need you.

So have a looky-loo at Melissa. You don't know her, but you know a girl like her. She's strong. She's confident. A good student. A great athlete. Hot. An all-around great girl. She's also totally independent. **She can do anything you can do, only better**. She doesn't need a guy to help her carry her books or to fix her car. She can take care of it all. She is her own woman. She's strong enough to open the door for herself, thank you very much. She doesn't want anyone to think she is **weak and dependent**, especially a guy. So she acts totally strong and *independent*. She has lots of guy friends. And girly stuff grosses her out. You get the pic? Normal, everyday girl.

So my question to you and whoever's reading over your shoulder is, why isn't she getting any dates? And when she does, why don't they last very long? Why won't a guy stick around for our little hottie?

66

Justin interruption (as predicted): Allow me to intrude here for a brief moment and provide the testosterone relief needed to answer this more-than-obvious question. Why doesn't Melissa have a guy? Hmmm . . . let me think real quick . . . **because she doesn't need one.** I mean, what would a guy do in her life? She's got it all under control. She does everything herself that we, as guys, would normally like to do for her.

Hayley: So Melissa's major boyfriend void is because she's her own man? Okay, makes sense. But she has no idea that that's why she's dateless.

Justin: Well, if she reads this book, she will. So why all the jabbering about Melissa?

Hayley: I love you, too, smart mouth. It's because looking at girls will tell us a lot about you guys. I know, here comes the girl, getting all deep and psycho on ya. But just roll up your pants and keep walking. When you first read about Melissa, what was your reaction? Good, bad? Hot, not?

Justin: If you're a guy like me, your first thought is, bingo! That's my kind of girl. Athletic, hot, independent—she's mine.

Hayley: Okay, so now fast-forward 3 months. You got her, you've been together for a while, and she's still the same athletic, competitive, independent girl as always. **She doesn't need you,** and everyone knows it. She is in control of her life, the relationship, and even you. So now how do you feel?

Justin: Again, if you're like me, you're gone. The initial hotness is gone because she doesn't need a guy around for *anything.* There's no challenge, no spark, nothing.

Hayley: Gotcha. Okay, so here's the mix-up as I see it. We become this independent, I-don't-need-you kind of girl because we think this impresses you. And initially this might be true, but what we don't get is that what's initially attractive—the guy qualities like independence and competitiveness—turns out to be the reason you lose interest? It's like you wake up one day

67

and *bam!* you realize that she's just a guy friend with extra padding? I'm following you here. But to that I say fine, she needs to learn how to be a woman—but then I have to add that **you guys have to learn how to be men.** Is that too harsh?

Justin: No, keep goin', you're on an estrogen roll.

Hayley: Okay, well, the way I see it, time has changed us. Back in the prehistoric days before MTV, guys knew how to be men and girls knew how to be women. Caveman Bob would go out and hunt the meal down and bring it back, and the woman would take the beast feast of the day and do amazing things with a baster and spatula made of flint. She would make meals, make clothes, make jewelry. It was perfect. They worked independently, but each totally depended on the other. Even in the days of your great-grandparents, the men went out and worked the cattle while the women took care of the house, the garden, the kids, and the domestic animals. Nowadays we all go out and hunt the next computer screen and turn it on. The roles are blurred.

And you know something? I don't think that God made us to be islands, all self-sustaining, guys and girls doing their own thing, not needing the other. **He made us to be interdependent.** Each of us doing our own thing but still **dependent on each other**. He made it so that our girl-weaknesses, the things we aren't good at, are filled by your guy-strengths and versa-versa.

And I can say this 'cuz I'm a girl: I think the trouble started with the sexual revolution of the '60s, when women decided it was just as easy for us to do what you men usually did. And it's true, **we can do it**. But slowly we started taking on more and more male roles while keeping our female roles, too. Ugh, too many roles. Too little time. All the while the men sat back and let this happen. And as a result you all became needed less and less. And suddenly average girls like Melissa have become so independent that they will never need a guy.

Justin: Wow, deep thoughts with Hayley Morgan. That's good, H, so now let me spew out some verbiage. Fellas, it's time to take back our position as men. No more walking around like a beat-down wimp. Stand up and be a man. This is what I want you to do. Sit back, ponder, and then pick up your pencil.

How can we step up and take back our roles as men? _____

_____

In today's society, what are male roles? _____

If you are doing this with more dudes, compare notes. Find ways to start being men.

Be a Gentleman

Hayley: That was cool. Thanks for saying that, Justin. It's true, we need guys to be men and help us girls get back to being, well, girls. (That wasn't really a blonde moment; it's just hard to explain it and sound intelligent.) The trouble is that girls—and I'm the first to admit it—are very hard to understand. It's like we have our own language or something.

Justin: You do.

Hayley: Okay, so what if I, as a girl, were to share some Girleeze lessons with you? (Girleeze is the language spoken in the well-known but little-understood country of Girland.) Would that help you in your quest for twoo wuv?

Justin: Lay it on, sister. Wait, lemme get a pen. . . . Okay, go.

Hayley: All right, here goes, the truth about what girls really want. Don't let the girls know I told you this, but the #1 thing we are really looking for, no matter how much we say we aren't, is

69

a knight in shining armor. In the olden days he was easy to find. I mean, he was a knight, and, well, his armor was shiny. But alas, today it's a little harder to find your knight. We still want him, but we can't recognize him as easily as we used to because the uniform changed over the centuries. But the concept is still there. Now before you run off and start reading *Sleeping Beauty*, let me tell you about the modern-day knight in shining armor's to-do list for the modern-day girl.

☐ 1. *Rescue maiden from castle*

Deep in our DNA, we girls feel the need to be special, important, and cared for. In the days of dragons and knights, that meant being saved by Prince Charming from the evil lord who locked you away in his castle. That's not happening so much nowadays, but Prince Charm' can still show up. "How?" I can hear you ask. It's easy.

Think castle.

Think rescue.

Think go pick her up.

At her door!

Whatever you do, don't drive up to her house and honk—bad prince, bad, bad prince! Don't *meet* her at the movie, or anywhere for that matter. **Go to her house, pick her up,** and at the end of the night **walk her all the way back to her front door.** This isn't so you can score a sloppy good night kiss; it's because she is precious cargo. Would you throw $1,000 in the front yard and just assume that it made it into the house? If so, send your money to I Am Stupid, P.O. Box 832, Stupidville, TN 37306. The girl is more valuable than any amount of cash, so make sure you deliver her all the way back to the door.

The bonus here is that you will start setting yourself apart as the knight in shining armor. She might not get it right away, but her DNA will stand up straight and take notice. And soon her heart will find a reason to love you.

☐ 2. Protect her honor

Knights had the honor thing down. Everything was a matter of honor and character. His knighthood depended on it. So what's that look like today? It looks like protecting her honor. Obvious honor-breaker: sex. Controlling yourself is a major part of honor, and check this out: *"But among you there must not be even be a hint of sexual immorality, or of any kind of impurity"* (Eph. 5:3 NIV). This means don't put her in situations that could be questionable to whoever hears about it or sees it. Like going to the lake so you can "be alone and talk"—yeah, right. Or the two of you being alone in your room with the door shut. Even with people at home, it looks bad. Think about the **"hint"** part of "not a **hint** of sexual immorality." Don't blow her honor by creating a hint of sexual immorality for her.

☐ 3. Go off to War

Now, boys, don't run off and join the army so you can become the knight. In the modern world this isn't about fighting. It's about adventure. It's about living life to the fullest. All that stuff Justin talked about earlier. Get out, get involved, make a difference, and share that with the girl.

☐ 4. Escort her to the ball

Every good knight-and-princess story has a fairy-tale ball. This is where the knight really gets to shine and make the girl feel like the princess of her dreams. For you this could be a dance or even a date, and it goes like this:

71

- Open the door. Not for yourself, for her. In fact, I told the girls to stand there until you do open it, so now you have to. It's not that a girl can't open the door. It's about you stepping out in front of her as the knight and taking care of her. (Justin: One comment here: Get ready for the block. A lot of girls are overly independent types who will put up the argument that they can do it themselves. My fave response to that is, "I didn't open it because you're a woman. I opened it because I'm a man." This works with car doors as well.)

- Pull out her chair. Not like some junior high prank. Push it back in when she sits down. It's a small gesture that lets her know she's important.

- Stand up. When she gets up to go to the restroom or wherever, you stand up. When she comes back, again, stand up. It's just an honor thing.

- Learn to dance. Most guys get left behind on this one. Either you're too embarrassed or you just don't know how. And I'm not talking about some head-banging, body-jumping kind of dancing. I'm talking about slow dancing. It's not that hard. All you have to do is hold the girl and move back and forth to the music. You don't have to be a pro. Just do it with confidence and attitude, and you will be the knight. (Go-the-extra-mile note: If you really want to be a chick magnet, take ballroom dance lessons. Believe me, they will come in handy many times in your dating life.)

- Know how to communicate. The problem with the princess is that she speaks a totally different language than the knights. So here's a few talk-tips that will take you to shiny-knight status.

    1. Eyes have their own language. We just love it when you look us in the eyes when you talk. In fact, if

72

you don't look us in the eyes, we assume you aren't listening. That's bad. We have no clue why you don't look us in the eyes when we talk to you. Guys can talk to each other and never even see each other's eyes and it's cool, but not for us. We need face-to-face time. So when you sit somewhere, always turn your body so she can see your whole face. She'll love it.

2. Use your ears. The princess bonds to the prince who listens to her. She bonds by talking, so listen. At all costs, listen. She *will* shut up eventually.

3. Anticipation = good thing. Girls love to look forward to stuff. Wanna score major prince points? Call her at least 4 days before the big date. This gives her time to tell all her friends, do her hair and nails, shop, and do all the essential things of Girland. The more anticipation the better.

4. Flowers speak volumes. Girls want to know they are the object of your affection, and flowers do the job nicely. Don't make 'em all serious like 12 red roses. Go pick some wildflowers and put a ribbon around 'em. Or buy some daisies and wrap them in newspaper. Be creative. She'll love it.

5. Nothing wrong = something wrong. If you ask her what's wrong and she says, "I don't know" or "Nothing," that means there really is something wrong. I know, this makes no sense to you, I've heard. But it makes perfect sense to us. If we say, "I don't know," that means you should ask us more about what's wrong so we know you really care. So don't give up when she says nothing's wrong. Chances are there's something wrong.

By the way, get ready to be grilled by a girl when you tell her nothing is wrong. She thinks that means, "Ask me more about what's wrong, 'cuz I just wanna know

73

you wanna talk about it." So don't get mad when she keeps pushing you to find out what's wrong.

Justin: Wait a minute, wait a minute, it sounds like you just confirmed that girls are nuts. They don't even mean what they say. This is freaky!

<u>Hayley:</u> I know, it's hard news to hear for the first time. But trust me, once you get this stuff down, your life will be like butta. Smooooth! You have two options: Keep on misinterpreting what we do and say or learn the language and join in with the native Girlanders. It's much easier to get along in a country when you speak the language. So learn the language, and life will be great for all of us.

Justin: Thanks for the info. Well, guys, you ready to practice? I am. All this stuff we've been digging into isn't to help you score with the latest hot chick; this stuff is about honoring women and learning to love them the way they want to be loved. So make sure that whatever you learned here today, you practice often. Get the door for old women, young women, ugly women, and hot women. Stand up when any woman at your table goes to the bathroom. Be a respecter of women, and you will get rewards for the rest of your life.

So starting now, make the change. Don't try to do all this stuff at once. You'll get overloaded and give up. Start with one thing, like opening the door. Do that all week. Make it an automatic part of who you are. Then move to something else, like pulling out the chair, and then to standing up. It will make you feel like more of a man, and to her you will be mega-impressive.

THE DATE

by Hastin Morgadoo + Juyley Lookagan — the Alligator Hunters

In the *Dateable* kingdom live two integral yet different members of the species: the male, who is the aggressor, the hunter, the provider; and the female, who is the nurturer, the talker, the emoter. The *Dateable* ecosystem needs one male and one female of the species for successful dating.

To help you better understand the *Dateable* ecosystem, we have provided in the pages to follow a thorough breakdown of the dating ritual between male and female human beings. Readers will kindly note that any description of the reader is purely coincidental, as we are investigating the species in general. So without further ado, we have the *Dateable* kingdom.

The Double-take

When the male of the species attempts to attract a mate, the first and most important action is the double-take. This is when the male and female see one another and are so alarmed by each other's beauty that they look away in embarrassment but must look back again because the attraction is so strong. The double-take is a surefire sign that the female is interested in the male. And the male can use the double-take as a nifty clue to alert the female to his interest. But the male must be careful not to overdo it, or the female will feel like she's being gawked at by construction workers on lunch break. Thus the subtle

75

look, then a clever movement of the eyes back to another part of the room, a 3-second pause, and then the returning of his sensitive eyes to the female will let the female know that the male is interested.

the Chase ⟵

If the female signals the male of her receptiveness by returning the male's gentle stare with a smile or an eye lock, then the male can proceed to give chase to his prey. In this delicate maneuver, the male establishes his interest even more definitely by approaching the female for conversation. He makes every effort to satisfy the female's need for communication and listens to her as she talks about herself. In this stage the male's goal is to let the female know that she is his choice, his goal. She must become the sole focus of his chasing efforts if he wants to reap the rewards of the catch.

Note: If the female shows absolutely no interest in any of the male's advances, then the successful male stops the process here. He knows that to chase a prey not interested in being caught is bad form.

the phone call

When the healthy male discovers that the female is interested in him, he then ventures further from his cave and makes the next advance: the phone call. When the male makes this phone call, he is polite, conversational, and inquisitive. He asks her questions about her life and pretends to be interested even if he isn't. He never monopolizes the conversation, even if the female asks him a lot of questions. He makes sure that she feels fully bonded by being allowed to talk. At the end of the call the male is allowed to ask to call her again or even to ask if he can take her out at least 4 days later.

76

Special Note on Asking Her Out: The *Dateable* male always assumes that the female is in demand, and therefore he never asks her out for the same day he is calling, unless there is a large group going and it would be appropriate to invite the female along. He allows the female to totally prepare for and dream about the date that will be just between the two of them.

The male who chooses to disregard this piece of advice should get used to becoming very bored with said female. When he realizes there was never a chase, his male nature will kick in and the female in question will become less desirable day by day.

the date

To make it easier for the nonspecialist in the field to understand the next phase of the dating ritual, we have included a list of rules that better explain the Date. Male-female outings in the *Dateable* kingdom must follow these strict rules.

Rule #1: Whoever asks, drives. The smart male knows that the female is the prize. Therefore the clever male asks, pays, drives, and leads. So the smart male insists on picking her up, even if it is out of his way. He never offers to meet her, because he knows that the female desires to be treated with great care and the harder he works, the more she likes him.

Note: If the male isn't old enough to drive, he isn't old enough to date.

Habitat Side Note: If subjects live in a major city with public transportation, the male goes directly to the door to pick up the female and never makes her meet him at the station. He returns her to said location at the end of the outing.

Rule #2: Dateable males always get doors. The *Dateable* male moves out ahead of the female in order to get to the door before the female does. Then he opens it and allows her to enter before him.

Note: He doesn't walk in front of her when they walk; he only speeds up to get in front of her at the door.

Rule #3: Dateable males plan. They know before they approach the female for the date where they will be going. They might play the rest of the date by ear, but the *Dateable* male never puts

77

the burden on the female to decide where to go. He wants to take care of her in everything.

Rule #4: Whoever asks, pays. The female's need to be cared for is met when the hunter-gatherer male pays for the date.

Note: If he is not ready to pay, then he is not ready to date her.

Rule #5: The *Dateable* male does not ask for or take a kiss good night, nor does he try to touch the female's body inappropriately. He remembers that she is unique, important, priceless, and to be honored.

The Next Day

The truly *Dateable* male calls the female the next day to thank her for the date. He might even put a card in her locker thanking her for a great evening. Then he is sure to call her again a few days later to catch up and to continue the dating ritual with her. The *Dateable* female loves to be called just to talk within 4 or 5 days of the last date.

The truly *Dateable* male is successful in learning the rituals and practices of the female in the *Dateable* kingdom. He is responsive to her needs and does all he can to meet them in an attempt to please her. He understands that the *Dateable* female has a different language than the male, and as such he makes every effort to understand her and her entire species. As a result the *Dateable* male becomes a successful and fulfilled man as he conquers the dating process and learns to serve others in the *Dateable* kingdom.

DATE NIGHT

DINNER AND A MOVIE

It's Date Night again. My how time flies, huh? So what shall we do tonight? Maybe dinner and a movie? A bit more ho-hum than last week. Or is it? Here's Part 1: food. Doesn't have to be fancy, just has to be a place where they seat you and serve you. Your first job is to take care of the girl (of all the girls, if you're in a group). Your second job is to care for everyone else. Real men aren't jerks. They serve people and care for them. And that means your server, the bus boy, whoever you come into contact with. Care about them. Treat them like humans. Treat them like God's precious kids. How? Here are some pointers:

- Find out their name and tell them yours. You are, after all, all God's kids. They aren't your slaves.
- Respect the fact that they have a hard job, and give them a break.
- Be friendly. Care about them.
- Don't get upset if they get your food wrong or late. (Note: You can certainly say something, but not in an angry way.)
- Smile at them.
- Leave them a big tip. (You don't have to do this every time. Just muster all you can today and do it. Did you know that Christians are known in the food industry as the worst tippers? That means that servers hate serving Christians. You are God's representative. Represent him as best you can. Be generous. Don't tell them it's from Jesus; just love them like Jesus would. Their spirits will know, and their hearts will be lifted.)

Now about the girl(s) in your life: Your job is to serve her. As guys we are programmed to take care of women, and the

79

amazing thing is that they are programmed to be taken care of. They love it. And they love the guys who do it. So that means get her chair for her and push it in as she sits. Stand up when she gets up to go the ladies' room. Treat her special. You can also ask her what she'd like to eat and order it for her. And wanna earn extra points? Here's a tip: If the girl is upset about wrong orders, late waiters, or anything to do with the food, then you, as the man who takes care of things, won't get all uptight with her 'cuz she complained. Agree with her. She likes it when you agree with her. Then say, "If they don't come soon, I'll go find someone to take care of it." Treat her like the princess she is, and she will find you more and more attractive.

Part 2: after dinner, a movie. For this pick a movie that might actually have a substantial plot. Something besides the sequel to *American Pie* or anything Tom Green. Maybe a remake of an old film. Or a drama. Historical movies are great. Even a great animated film would be good, since they are loaded with content. If you want to try a rental, then here are some good ones to start with: *Bruce Almighty, Finding Nemo, The Count of Monte Cristo, The Matrix, Shrek, Gladiator, The Shawshank Redemption, The Hurricane, Signs, Dead Man Walking.*

Your goal: Find Jesus in the film. After the film go to a coffee shop or back home and talk about your thoughts on the spiritual impact of the film. If you can't find a symbol of Jesus or his life, then find the biblical message. Every film has one. **God is everywhere there is substance.** If you can't find God in the film, then find where it's missing God. Ask questions like this:

80

- What was the moral?
- Was there any faith in the characters' lives? What was their faith in?
- How did they try to control their happiness?
- What was their fatal flaw that would keep them from Christ?
- How did they resemble a believer?
- What was missing from their lives (besides the obvious answer of Christ)?
- What did they need more than anything to lead them to Christ?
- How did their sin keep them in turmoil?
- How would a relationship with Christ have changed their lives?
- If God wasn't real to the characters, then why? What kept them separate from him?

That should get you going. Spend a good 30 minutes talking about the movie. Find God in it. Find him in as much of the movie as you can. And don't ever miss God in anything. He is everywhere. Everything points back to him.

81

You did it. Dance around like a little monkey. You made it through the month and have become the most *Dateable* guy on the planet (okay, on the little planet in your mind). And now it's time to par-tay! Hopefully you've been working on this for 3 weeks and you are cranked and ready to go! But here's a little recap of what this *Dateable* Bash will involve:

> Quiz Your *Dateability*
> Walk Down Memory Lane – news report, slide show, photo album, lots of laughs
> Awards Ceremony – the good, the better, the totally *Dateable*
> Fun – eat, talk, laugh, have a ball

First things first! Now, just to find out how far you've come on the *Dateable* journey, we've got a parting quiz for you. Let's see if you've really learned anything at all. Take it—that is, if you aren't too scared of failing!

Quiz: What do you know about Girls now?

1. When it comes to asking a girl out, I:
   a. still think it's easier when she asks me
   b. am ready to be brave enough to make the first move
   c. wait to see if she's showing the signs of flirting, then when I know for sure she likes me, I'll start a convo with her

2. The last time I was with a girl, I:
   a. talked her ear off

82

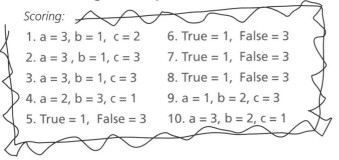

  b. asked her lots of questions and found out a lot about her

  c. I let her talk, almost fell asleep, but she seemed to really want to talk

3. Which term best describes girls?
  a. hunters
  b. shoppers
  c. pains in the pattoot

4. Which statement would a girl rather hear at the end of a date?
  a. You have such good taste in movies
  b. That was a great idea; thanks for planning the date
  c. I loved the movie

5. If you ask, you pay.   True   False

6. If she's carrying something, you offer to help carry it for her.   True   False

7. I'm willing to take risks in life.   True   False

8. When I am talking to someone, I always look them in the eye.   True   False

9. Girls prefer:
  a. adventure
  b. activities
  c. advice

10. When a girl is cold, I:
  a. ask her why she didn't bring warmer clothes
  b. offer to take her home
  c. give her my coat or sweater

Scoring:

1. a = 3, b = 1, c = 2   6. True = 1, False = 3
2. a = 3 , b = 1, c = 3   7. True = 1, False = 3
3. a = 3, b = 1, c = 3   8. True = 1, False = 3
4. a = 2, b = 3, c = 1   9. a = 1, b = 2, c = 3
5. True = 1, False = 3   10. a = 3, b = 2, c = 1

83

10–15: Dear *Dateable* Grad, *you did it! You read the book, you passed the class, and you're ready to go on to* **Dateable** *Greatness. Your love life should be all that plus a side order of bacon!*

16–20: Almost *Dateable*. *Well, what can I say? You read the book. You did the focus groups. You had the dates. But still not too sure it really all makes sense? That's okay. Give it some time. Read the book again. Try out some of the stuff we suggest. Results will come; it's just a matter of time.*

21–30: Did you read the same book? *Where did we go wrong? Did you remember to read the guys' side and not the girls'? Maybe take another trip down* **Dateable** *Lane. A second read might do you good. Or heck, just keep doing what you've been doing— you're sure to keep getting what you've been getting!*

Once you've done the Quiz, you can party on with all the other cool stuff you planned. Save the serious business, "Commit to the List," to do later on your own. This is the time to let loose and enjoy the success of a hard journey. Yep, girls are still crazy. Yep, you will still do stupid stuff. But now you understand a little more about what is *really* going in the guy/girl world.

If you've loved this *Dateable* month and the way you've grown with your group, then keep the feeling alive. Plan a "Dinner at 8" once a month. What's that, you say? Glad you asked. You're so good like that. Dinner at 8 is just what it sounds like. It's dinner and it's at 7:00 (just kidding, it really is at 8:00). Get your gang together once a month and go out. Plan something fun for the girls. Open doors and pull out chairs. Be *Dateable!* It's a blast! If you're committing to do this, then get on **www.RUDateable.com** and let us know. We'd love to find out what's going on and how your Dinner at 8 works. We also want photos. You can submit your photos from your *Dateable* Bash newscast and any other photos you shoot from then on. We'll keep the rest of the world posted on your *Dateable* journey!

ON YOUR OWN — the SOLO WRAP-UP

Commit to the List

It's time to really get serious about who you are as a man and a full-on *Dateable* Dude. Make the *Dateable* attitude a part of who you are—"Commit to the List."

This commitment is between you and your God. He knows what is in your heart, and he will help you stick to your commitment. So after you read the list of *Dateable* Rules and agree with them, in the space given write him a prayer that tells him why you want to Commit to the List. Be sure to sign it. That's your word. Then your job, besides staying committed, is to tell at least one other person about your *Dateable* commitment. This puts you on the right path for becoming who God wants you to be—a powerful, adventurous, *Dateable* Man.

the dateable rules (for Guys)

1. Being a Guy Is Good – *Dateable* guys know that they aren't as sensitive as girls and that's okay. They know that they are stronger, more dangerous, and more adventurous and that's okay too. *Dateable* guys are real men who aren't afraid to be guys.

2. Believe in Yourself – *Dateable* guys know they are men even if someone has tried to bring them down or make them less than men. They know that the past doesn't define the future.

85

3. Control Your Mind – *Dateable* guys know that God demands self-control. They learn ways to control their minds so they can control their bodies.

4. Don't Just Want a Win, Want an Adventure – *Dateable* guys know life is about danger. You might not win, but that's not the point—*doing* it is. *Dateable* guys risk failure to live the adventure of life.

5. Face Your Fears – *Dateable* guys will not be controlled by fear. Whatever controls you, owns you. Fear is from the enemy, so the *Dateable* guy stands in the face of it and says, "Bring it on!"

6. Men of God Are Wild, Not Domesticated – *Dateable* guys aren't tamed. They don't live by the same rules as the opposite sex. They fight battles, conquer lands, and stand up for the oppressed.

7. Read God into It. – *Dateable* guys read God into it. They ask, "What would he say if he could talk to me through this situation?"

8. Be Honest with Girls – *Dateable* guys don't use the truth to their advantage. They know that girls read into things, so they don't use that for their own good. They are honest and not manipulative.

9. Be a Gentleman – Chivalry is not dead with the *Dateable* guy. Even if society thinks this is old-fashioned, he knows that it is God-fashioned. He keeps his gentleman's side strong and considers all women important enough to care for.

10. Keep It Covered Up – *Dateable* guys know that porn is bad for the spirit and the mind. They keep women covered up.

If you agree with the Rules, you are ready to Commit to the List. Here it is:

As a *Dateable* guy, I will
1. stand up like a real man
2. not lie to you or for you
3. control how far we go
4. open doors and pull out chairs
5. know it will not last

Dear God,

_____

_____

_____

_____

_____

_____

_____

_____

_____

Name

Justin Lookadoo—the name says it all. He's a freak, let's just be frank. But even freaks can have a point, and Justin's is sharp enough to cut your heart out and serve it to you on a platter. He has an amazing ability to take simple truth and make you say, "Duh, why didn't I think of that?" And with this simple truth he'll turn your world upside down.

Justin has been doing this kind of stuff from stages for the past 12 years, yes, since he was just a pup. He was a juvenile probation officer for 5½ years in the toughest part of East Texas. And just a few years ago he left the jail business to tour the U.S., speaking in public schools and at leadership conferences like MADD, DARE, and FFA. He speaks all over the country, so if you want him in your school or church, check out his web site for more info. Hopefully some day you'll get to see the tall one in person and allow him to Lookadoo ya.

In the meantime, check out one of his many books out there. He wrote *Step Off, The Hardest 30 Days of Your Life*. And boy, is it. Don't try this one unless you are prepared to work your butt off in the wildest adventure you've ever had. He also wrote *Extreme Encounters,* a year-long devotional that doesn't scold you as much as *Step Off*. Oh, and yeah, there's also *Ask Hayley/Ask Justin,* a really rockin' book that answers all those freaky questions you might have about dating, love, sex, and the opposite sex.

Hayley Morgan is just plain cool. What else can we say? She's got an answer for everything. Maybe that's why they published *Ask Hayley/Ask Justin*, so people could hear some of her words of wisdom. Wherever she goes, students line up to ask her about their relationships and their futures.

She probably learned a lot of her stuff from her trippy life. She has lived in Europe, speaks fluent French, toured for 4 months with a French theater troupe, performing in 8 countries and in 3 languages. She visited the orphans in India and performed in front of 1000s of children in that country.

She worked for a little shoe company called Nike out in rainy Portland, Oregon, until she got so sick of being wet and up and moved to Nashville, Tennessee, where she now hangs her hat. She created and developed a line of books and Bibles for teenagers called Extreme for Jesus. Perhaps you've heard of the Extreme Teen Bible that started the whole thing. After selling over 2 million books with Thomas Nelson, Hayley left corporate America to slow down and write books like *Dateable* and spend her spare time talking to teens across the country. She also wrote *Extreme Encounters,* the book that Justin claims to have written. But once you've talked to both of them, you'll understand who the real brains of the team is.

the dateable rules

a guide to the sexes

Girl's Side

Justin Lookadoo
and Hayley Morgan

Fleming H. Revell
A Division of Baker Book House Co
Grand Rapids, Michigan 49516

Library of Congress Cataloging-in-Publication Data is on file at the Library of
Congress, Washington, D.C.

ISBN 0-8007-5915-X (pbk.)

Published in association with Yates and Yates, LLP, Literary Agents, Orange,
California.

Scripture marked NIV is taken from the HOLY BIBLE, NEW INTERNATIONAL
VERSION®. NIV®. Copyright © 1973, 1978, 1984 by International Bible Society.
Used by permission of Zondervan. All rights reserved.

Scripture marked NLT is taken from the *Holy Bible*, New Living Translation, copyright © 1996. Used by permission of Tyndale House Publishers, Inc., Wheaton,
IL 60189. All rights reserved.

Scripture marked MESSAGE is taken from THE MESSAGE. Copyright © by Eugene
H. Peterson 1993, 1994, 1995. Used by permisison of NavPress Publishing
Group.

Cover photo of TV sets by Adri Berger/Getty Images

Interior design by Brian Brunsting

GiRLS (SECTION)
Contents

No GUYS ALLOWED!!

FLiP to your own Side, fellas.

T h e   O w n e r ' s   M a n u a l

This is a book. But it's more than one book—it's really two books glued together and sold as one book. It doesn't get any better than that! Unless of course you live in a grass hut in Hawaii and play in the ocean all day. That's pretty cool too. But getting back to our book, we call it Flip. Well, really we call it a flip book, but you can call it Flip for short. That means **one side** is written **for girls** and the **other** is written **for guys.** For those of you who are already confused, that means that if you pee standing up, you're reading the wrong side.

To help you better utilize your two books in one, we have provided these easy-to-follow directions in both English and Japanese. (We really don't know Japanese but what's an owner's manual without it?) Make sure you have all of the parts required to operate this book before proceeding. See the list of parts below:

- Book
- Pen (not included)
- Bible (not included)
- Vital information (partially included)
- Focus Group Members (not included)
- Date Night (ideas included, date not included)
- Blank spaces (provided for your writing pleasure)

- 本
- ペン（含まれません）
- 聖書（含まれません）
- 重要な情報（一部含まれます）
- フォーカス・グループ・メンバー（含まれません）
- デート・ナイト（アイディアは含まれますが相手は含まれません）
- 余白スペース（自由にお書きください）

4

Follow these simple steps to maximize your *Dateable Rules* experience:

1. Read the book. If that's too vague, don't worry—you can resort to the "How to Read This Book" directions at the beginning of each week. If you decide not to follow the HRTB directions, then please finish the week by the end of the week.

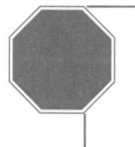

2. Underline things. Underlining is good, unless of course you're a member of the ICA (Ink Conservationists Association). But since they don't date, they probably aren't reading this book. In any case, underlining will help you quickly locate and distribute information to the guys you are doing the book with.

3. Date Night. It's the night you date. You date either the guy or the group of guys you are doing this book with. Hmm, that sounded completely wrong. Let me rephrase: Date Night is a night for everyone who is doing the book together to get together and go out, whether it's a couple or a whole group. Be sure to read all the articles for that week before advancing to Date Night. The goal of the Date Night will all become clear by then.

1. 初めに言ったはずです。本を読んでください。次に、前文をもう一度読んでください。

2. まだがんばって読もうしてるのですか。これは教科書ではなく、デートに関する本なんです。訳そうなんて無駄な努力はやめて、実践してください。

3. まだ訳しているようですね。もう3つ目。そろそろデート・ナイトに移ってもいいのでは？さあ、がんばって！

4. Focus Group. The Focus Group happens on the final day of the week. Please refer to "Legal Mumbo Jumbo" (it's not hard to find; it's on the next page) for more information on the purpose of said Focus Group. Basically it's a group of people who get together to talk. That's all we have to say about that for now.

4. おめでとう。この本にあるすべての日本語の翻訳に成功しました。もちろん最後の文節を訳したとしたら大間違い。最初に戻って、もう一度がんばってください。

Important Safety Tips

To reduce the risk of electrical shock, never read this book while operating a toaster while taking a bath.

4 out of 5 dentists surveyed didn't read this book but did recommend brushing with fluoride toothpaste twice daily to prevent tooth decay.

Do not read this book while driving a motorized vehicle or operating heavy machinery.

Kickoff Focus Group

Wouldn't it be cool if you could **do a focus group on *your* "target audience"—guys**? Wouldn't it be amazing to just pick their brains? To find out what goes on in there, if anything? I mean, what *are* they thinking? It would be like being that fly on the wall listening to all their private conversations. Wouldn't it be great? Well, dream no more. Today your dream has become a reality. Before you lift another *Dateable* finger, you're gonna do a little **Focus Group of your own.** You girls and your target audience, the group of guys you do this study with, will get to ask each other questions about stuff you just don't have a clue about—the opposite sex. You are going to get together and focus before you go any further in the book. If you are doing this study with your crush, you're gonna find out some stuff about each other that you never understood.

What do guys want? My my, don't we all want to know. They can seem impossible to figure out. So to get started, girls, you are

7

going to take a little quiz to see how well you understand guys. Then you'll take 5 minutes as a group to **write down 5 things you want to know about guys**. And, you guessed it, the guys are going to be able to ask you 5 things they've always wanted to know about you. Nothing's sacred. Ask anything: "What do you like in girls?" "Why do you act like a dork whenever your guy friends are around?" "How come you don't want to talk when you're mad?" Stuff that you've always wanted to ask but been too afraid to. (Duh Note: If there are 30 of you doing this Focus Group, you still only get to ask 5 questions. Get it? Too many people. Too many questions. Too little time. Choose the best ones.)

Now, once you've got your Qs, it's time for the Q&A part of the Focus Group. If it's just you and your crush, get somewhere quiet and go through the questions. If you're a group, then here's your deal: Get all the guys on one side of the room facing the girls, who are on the other side of the room. **Get a moderator**, someone who can read the questions and **run the timer**. Each side gets up to **5 minutes to answer each question.** That's the limit. For some questions it might only take a sec, but for others there will be lots of blabbin' once the answer comes out. **Get a dry-erase board** or something else to make your notes on. (It can serve as evidence in the lawsuits you might end up bringing against each other.)

At the end of your time, you will have what focus groups for MTV and Coca-Cola pay thousands of dollars for: a real slice of Americana. The truth about the opposite sex—or is it?

DATEABLE Bash Plan

Okay, we're jumping way ahead here, but we have to, because in the last Focus Group you are going to get your party on. It's going to be the *Dateable* Bash. But to make it happen, you have to start doing things now. Like today. So before you begin the

8

journey, you're going to see how the story ends so you can plan the final blowout.

Here's the breakdown to get you rolling.

The *Dateable* Bash Planning Team: At the end of this book, you're going to get to throw a party. But we all know it takes time to plan a good party. So today we're going to get teams together so the party will hop and not flop. After you've done your quiz, brainstorming, and Q&A, you're going to assign teams. You need to pick a News Crew, Award Team, Design Team, Party Team, and any other teams you think will help. These are the people who are going to pull this whole event together. If just you and your crush are doing this book, then you guys might only document the month with your journals and your cameras and then have a big dinner or some kind of get-together to remember your month.

Descrip of Each Team:

News Crew – On the last day of this adventure (i.e., at the end of this book), the News Crew will take you for a walk down memory lane. From news reports of the month to video footage and slide shows, the News Crew's job is to record the memories for everyone involved. This team can be any size and involve any number of jobs. Just a few to choose from are written below. Pick your team and then brainstorm about who will do what throughout the month. Also start to figure out how you will present your report on the last day. **Members of the News Crew:**

Anchor – This person will be the talking head. The one who will get up in front of everyone and lead the recap. You can play with this. Get a male and female and do it like *SNL* news or the *Today* show. Or just get one person to do it. Your job will be to take quotes, record events, and put together a heartfelt/funny presentation for your

9

group using all the cool info the rest of the Crew gets over the month.

Photog – This person is in charge of pics. Take 'em during the week, on Date Night, and during Focus Groups. Get all the action shots you can.

Videographer – Name says it all. Shoot the month. Catch people talking about Date Night, dating, focusing, all the stuff you will be doing throughout the month.

Writer – Writers write. Beautiful how that works, isn't it? So the writer for this project will take notes on everything that happens. Maybe write it like a journal or like a TV show. But keep track of the things that go on in your group and the stuff that people say.

Awards Team – This team's job is to figure out what kinds of awards will be given out at the *Dateable* Bash. Shop 'til you drop. Find small things that can be given to the people who will be voted for. Make a list of things people can win: "Most Dateable," "Most Improved Dater," "Most Likely to Get the Door for a Girl," "Most Likely to Shut Up and Be Mysterious," "Best Planner," "Best Complimentor." The list could go on and on. Your job is to decide on the awards, make ballots for everyone, figure out what prizes each winner will get, and set up for voting to take place on *Dateable* Bash night.

Design Team – This team's job can include any number of things. Create a photo album using the photos taken. Make a slide show and put it to music. Create poster boards to decorate the walls. Hang banners from the ceiling. Make the night memorable. Decorate away!

Party Team – If you're going to have a party, someone has to plan. This team's job is to make sure the party happens. Find drinks, food, music, whatever. Make the night a big bash. Find the location, band, actors, games, whatever you need to make

10

the night a blast. Make sure that you coordinate with the News Crew so that they have everything they need as far as electrical outlets, video screens, tables, and so on. Your job is really to coordinate everyone so that you all work together as one big team. You come up with the flow for the night. Figure out what happens when. Get with the Design Team to see what they need. Yep, you are the traffic cop of the deal.

This is all about the fun. When you make it through the book, you will deserve a party. It will be the perfect ending to your journey through *Dateability*.

So here's the plan for this *Dateable* Kickoff:

- **Quiz Time: "Do You Understand Guys?" (5 minutes)**
- **Brainstorm: Come up with 5 questions you want to ask the guys (5 minutes)**
- **Q&A: Girls and guys take turns asking each other the 5 questions (total 50 minutes max)**
- *Dateable* **Bash Party Planning**

Got it? Okay then, get crackin'. Take the "Do You Understand Guys?" quiz below and score your answers. It'll help you see what kind of questions you need to ask the guys.

Quiz: Do You Understand Guys?

1. When a guy asks you out, you:
   - a. let him pick you up
   - b. tell him you'll meet him there
   - c. decide where you want to go and tell him you'll just pick him up

11

2. When you get dressed in the morning, you:
   a. put on whatever you feel best in
   b. try things on over and over 'til you find just the right outfit that will get his attention
   c. put on sweats or basketball shorts—life is too short to worry about matching outfits and shoes

3. If you have a hard time opening your water bottle, you:
   a. ask your best friend to help you
   b. hand it over to the closest guy and say, "Would you mind opening this for me?"
   c. just twist as hard as you can 'til eventually you get it open—I mean, nothing is going to beat you!

4. When a guys calls you:
   a. you end the conversation first
   b. he ends the conversation first
   c. you wait 'til there is total silence and finally say, "Well, it's been nice talking to you"

5. When a guy opens the car door for you, you:
   a. reach over to his side and unlock his before he gets in the car
   b. smile and say thank you, but you don't reach over and unlock his door
   c. tell him, "I can get the door myself, thank you very much"

6. At a restaurant with a guy, you:
   a. never eat much, 'cuz you feel self-conscious when you eat
   b. order a big meal but only eat a few bites, to look dainty
   c. order a good sized meal and eat it all; food is good, and you like to eat it!

7. When you start crushing on a guy, you:
   a. try to be where he is as often as you can so he notices you
   b. tell your friend to tell him you like him
   c. just pray that he will ask you—you hate to flirt

12

8. If a guy friend you don't like romantically asks you on a date, you:
    a. tell him, "Sorry, I'm just not interested in you like that"
    b. say yes, because it's just too hard to say no
    c. tell him, "Bug off, you reject!"

9. When you are at a party, you:
    a. find all your girlfriends and spend the night gabbing with them
    b. find the guy you like and make conversation with him
    c. sit on the couch waiting for someone to come talk with you

10. If you are mad at your guy friend, you:
    a. give him the silent treatment 'til he asks you what's wrong
    b. give him a lecture about how not to hurt you
    c. tell him he hurt you and let him apologize or explain

Time to get your score. Add up all your points:

1. a = 1, b = 3, c = 3   6. a = 3, b = 3, c = 1
2. a = 2, b = 1, c = 3   7. a = 1, b = 2, c = 3
3. a = 2, b = 1, c = 3   8. a = 1, b = 3, c = 3
4. a = 1, b = 3, c = 2   9. a = 1, b = 3, c = 3
5. a = 2, b = 1, c = 3   10. a = 3, b = 3, c = 1

10–13: Good Reader. *Guys are an open book, and you love reading them. You really get guys. You know what they like and how to act around them. You are a catch. Guys are glad you are the way you are, so keep up the good work. Mr. Perfect is out there looking for you.*

14–25: Study up. *You've done your studying, but you still need to do your homework. You aren't totally clueless about guys, just an airhead sometimes. Concentrate. You can do this. Guys are different from girls—remember that and you'll be the talk of the town.*

26–30: Clueless about the Opposite Sex! *You came to the right place, sister. It's time to figure out guys. If you want to change your love life, then keep on reading.*

13

Week

one
one

...BEAUTIFUL Girl

How to Read This Book This Week		
	Monday	read "AccepT Your Girlyness" and "Tell IT Like IT Is"
	Tuesday	read "The SexiesT Thing on a Girl Is Happiness"
	Wednesday	Take The nighT off
	Thursday	read "Girls Don'T FighT OTher Girls—Ever" and "Believe in Your BeauTy"
	Friday	go on a DaTe NighT, "CiTy Bus"
	Saturday	Day off
	Sunday	do your Focus Group

Accept your Girlyness

by Justin Lookadoo ♡ ♡

Girls, before we go anywhere, you're gonna have to understand why you are so dang irresistible to guys. I don't think you really get how amazing you are, so before we go anywhere else on this trip, you need to hear a few things from this guy. Today I represent the guys in your life, and I'm going to fill you in on what goes on inside my head when I think of girls.

The biggest thing that I just love about girls is how soft your skin is. Mine's all rough and hairy, but yours is so soft that I just love it when it brushes up against me. And you know what makes your skin softer than mine? Your body has extra fat cells. The fat cells that you love to hate are really the reason for your soft skin that I love to love.

And believe it or not, I love the fact that you're emotional, because that gives me something that I don't have. It's an adventure I don't get to live on my own. Now, if you are psycho-overemotional, that's another issue. But emotions are so feminine and so not male that I love it. It's uncharted territory. It's a maze. It's a challenge. It's what makes you a girl and not a guy.

I love the way you talk. Three words in an e-mail can totally make a man feel like fighting a battle and rescuing a beauty. The kind and feminine things you say are stuff I would never get from my guy friends, and I need it. I need to hear your sweet words like "You're my hero," or "You're so strong." When an e-mail starts with "Hey, Doll," my face lights up. I know for sure it isn't one of my guy friends talking—that would be freaky!

16

I love the cute little clothes you wear. A guy would never be caught dead in ruffles, but on you it's so girly, and that makes it cute.

I love your eyes. They might be the same eyes a guy could have, but they look so much better in your head. I just love your eyes. Mascara and all. I love the way you flirt, the way you smile at me, the way your hair smells. I love that I'm stronger than you and that you need me to take care of and protect you. When you can't open the ketchup bottle and ask me to, gosh I love that. I just love it when you need my help. When somebody upsets you and you need to cry on my shoulder, oh, that's a good feeling. And I love the way your hand is so little that it can fit into mine.

I notice that a lot of girls get hung up on size. "My nose is too big!" "My feet are too big!" Let me just tell you here and now that there are no girls whose feet are too big! Telling me stuff like "My butt is too big, and I'm too fat" just annoys me. In fact—news flash—I don't think anything about you being too this or too that 'til you tell me, and then I'm just sick of hearing it. If you are one of those girls who says, "My eyes are ugly and brown. I want blue eyes," I say there are plenty of guys who love brown eyes, and that's not going to determine if a guy goes out with you or not anyway. Here's the whole problem as I see it: Every girl's _____ is too _____, and you fill in the blanks. Your straight hair is too straight; your curly hair too curly. You all spend your life thinking you're too this, that, or the other. Stop it! Quit saying all the negative stuff about yourself. When you do that, what you are doing is basically telling us guys that we are wrong. When you get upset when I say you're beautiful and say, "No, I'm not," you are calling me stupid. It doesn't matter what *you* think about you; let *me* think what I want to think. When you tell a guy he's wrong, you run him off. Why would a guy want to go out with a girl

17

who disagrees with everything he thinks? He wouldn't. A guy is not going to pick a loser to go out with, especially not a self-proclaimed one. So if you don't like guys to tell you nice things about yourself, don't tell him that. Just go handle your issue, 'cuz you've got one.

I know it's hard, but you have to listen to me when I tell you not to compare yourself to the girls you see in mags or on TV. From a guy's perspective, we don't care that you don't look like them. We pretty much know they're fake anyway. I mean, we'll be turned on by that stuff because we see it, but we are also turned on by you because you're there. We don't expect you to be the perfect supermodel; we just need you to be there. I mean, a girl will think she's ugly 'cuz she's comparing herself to every other girl. "She has bigger breasts than me." "Her hair is thicker." Straight up, I don't care! I don't compare girls. Believe it or not, I'm a hunter, not a shopper. You girls shop for guys by comparing them, trying different things about them to see if they fit or not. I don't. I like you because you are a girl, period, the end. I'm not comparing you to every other girl. Like my friend Ben says, "I'll probably never get married 'cuz I love all girls. There's something about every one of them that I love." We don't need you to be perfect in every little thing. I find something alarmingly beautiful in each one of you. Your laugh, your smile, your hands, your eyes, each one of you has one thing that is uniquely you and uniquely attractive. So lay off the comparison charts and let us love that stuff about you.

You just give us something that we can't get from guys. We could get all psychoanalytical about it and say it was from a bond with our mother, but it's just the way God made us. He made guys and girls to be able to do different things. From a guy's perspective, all that girly stuff that we don't understand, we really don't want to understand. We just like it. We are happy with your girlyness.

18

HEAVY Lifting
Where You Get Your Spiritual Workout

So, that said, here's your heavy lifting for the week. Your mission, should you choose to accept it, is to accept all the compliments you get. Smile and say, "Thank you." It might be harder than you think. No rolling your eyes. No saying, "No, I'm just too fat!" No disagreeing with your complimentor. Don't tell people they are wrong by rejecting what they think simply because you disagree.

If you are going through this book with a group, you girls also have to compliment each other all week and bust whoever denies the compliments.

To get you started on this weeklong adventure, I want you to do something. I want you to compliment yourself. Right here and right now, I want you to list the things that are uniquely girly about you. Things like your soft skin, long hair, and nice smell. All the things that make you appealing to guys. You might not think you're much right now, and you might not feel very girly, but try to imagine yourself that way, 'cuz deep down you are. And don't just put stuff about your body, put stuff about **your emotions, your caring nature, your intuition.** Cool stuff like that. **Make a list of all things girly.** Okay, ready? Then get to it.

- my height
- my eyes
- my smile
- how I encourage
- how I love/care
- how I hurt for others
- my soft skin
- my pretty toes

So, how was it? Did you think of things you never really thought about as being girl stuff? That's what's so cool. If you had a hard time thinking of stuff, don't sweat it. By the end of this book you'll have plenty of stuff you like about your girly self. **You are a girl and girls rock.**

19

Tell It like It IS

by Hayley Morgan

Girlyness review: Remember, this week has just turned into a gotcha party. You need to throw compliments at your friends as much as possible this week and see if they try to dodge 'em or catch 'em. "I love that shirt." "You are so smart." Compliment the other girls in your group, and remember to just take their compliments with "Thank you."

Now, before we can go any further, we have to agree on one major thing. If you read *Dateable*, then you remember the chapter called "<u>Girls Lie to Themselves to Get What They Want</u>." It's stupid, but true: **<u>We girls lie to ourselves on a daily basis.</u>** About guys, about other girls, and about ourselves.

"He didn't mean to be a jerk!"

"That girl is just a slut, and I'm gonna get even with her."

"No one likes me 'cuz I'm fat."

The list goes on. Lies you tell yourself to make yourself feel better or to feel justified. It's a load of puppy dung. So listen, **if you aren't ready to start <u>telling yourself the nasty little truth</u>, then you aren't ready to do this book.** Just drop it now while you still have your self-centeredness intact. Get away while your delusions are still your own. 'Cuz in this book there will be no lying to yourself, about him or about yourself. And now, to add the final nail that broke the camel's back, here is the **guido verso** (that's Italiano for guide verse, I think) that will take us all through this whole study: **Philippians 4:8–9.** Open

20

up your Bible, flip the pages, find it, and write it all down right here. If you don't do this, then this whole book is useless and your mind will become a worthless pile of mush.

Finally brethren, whatever things are true, whatever things are noble, whatever things are just, whatever things are pure, whatever things are lovely, whatever things are of good report, if there is anything praiseworthy and any virtue—meditate on these things. The things that you have learned and received and heard and saw in me, these do, and the God of peace will be with you.

Okay, so what does this verse mean? Put it in girl talk. How would you explain it to your best friend?

All the things that are good, pure, and holy, focus your mind on them, think about them. Then everything you know God does—do it.

If you're real quick, then you said to yourself, **"Hmm, Self, I think it means I'm not supposed to lie, because I'm only supposed to think about true stuff, good stuff, right stuff,** and all that." Congratulations! You're as smart as you are beautiful! See, most of your problems in life come from the way you think about things. That's exactly the point of this whole book. If you can honestly say, "I think about good stuff most of the time. My mind is totally obsessed with the truth. I don't try to make something out of nothing, crying about stuff that doesn't go my way," then hello, Mother Teresa. But **if you are a normal girl, then your life is more like a roller coaster than a flat Texas highway.** And all that emotional turmoil and resulting stupid stuff you do comes from one thing: lies. Not lies guys tell you but lies *you* tell you.

27

So here's the place where you decide who you're going to be for the rest of your life. **Are you going to be the girl who gets controlled by every situation,** imagining the worst, plotting against other girls, manipulating guys? **Or are you going to be a** *Dateable* **girl** who practices our guido verso no matter whato?

Look at the list below and cross out all the things that this verse doesn't let you get away with any longer.

~~lying to myself~~
~~lying to my friends~~
~~worrying about bad stuff~~
~~ditching people~~
~~thinking about girls I wish were gone~~
encouraging people
hoping for the best
trusting people
loving life
~~calling people names~~

You'd better have crossed out 6 things, sister!

Now take it a step further. I want you to write this verse everywhere—on your folders, your mirror, 3 x 5 cards, the back of your arm, everywhere—and have it memorized by the end of the week. Homework? Bummer! But it's crucial. It's super-crucial. **It's superucial!** So get to work. To quote one of my favorite writers, Unknown Author, "Today is the first day of the rest of your life." So get your butt in gear and make your life the dream you want it to be. It's all up to you, baby!

22

The Sexiest Thing on a Girl is Happiness

by Hayley Morgan

Another compliment check: Have you been pouring it on your friends? I want you to look at the first one you see today and say, "You are so beautiful." And make her accept it.

What about you? When you want to feel beautiful, what do you do? Dress up? Makeup up? Flirt 'til the cows come home? (Of course, the cows never actually *come* home; it's just a saying.) Think about it for a minute. **What do you do to feel beautiful?** I mean, really, **do you feel like a true beauty?** Do you feel like the perfect creature that guys are searching for? Do you look in the mirror and pose like a supermodel? Beautiful is a word that means a lot of different things to a lot of different people. But one thing is the same—every girl wants to be beautiful. So are you? Are you really beautiful? Have you been called beautiful? Maybe a lot of people or maybe hardly anyone you can think of thinks you are beautiful, but are you one of them? The cheesy, feel-good answer here is "It only matters if *I* think I'm beautiful." Problem is, *you don't,* do you?

Honest girls who answered "No," please read on. (The rest of you little liars, shut the book.)

Face it, feeling beautiful is something every girl is after. So how do you go about getting that feeling of beautiful? Think about what you do to make yourself feel pretty.

23

How do you act? _girly flirty, sexy_

What do you do? _work out_

What do you wear? _things that accentuate my figure_

What do you add to yourself to make yourself beautiful?
make-up, jewelry

Clothes Make the Beauty?

Let's look at one beauty add-on: clothes. Why do we buy clothes? Because we like 'em? Yeah, okay, but most importantly because **we look hot in them.** We're gearing up to catch the attention of a guy. We **want to be noticed.** So we buy clothes that will cover up the flaws and accentuate the goods. (Side note: If this isn't you, then you might have the opposite problem: fear of being beautiful. These girls do all they can to hide their beauty under baggy clothes and messy hair. Different package, same problem.)

Clothes shopping is really beauty hunting. We think that **somewhere in those racks and racks of clothes our beauty is waiting to be revealed.** We think that if you search long enough and try on quick enough, we can get the beauty before another girl beats us to it.

Now there's nothing wrong with hunting for your beauty. **It's natural to want to attract the opposite sex.** It's the nature thing. Boy chases cute girl and the species goes on. It's true, **guys are visual,** and that's part of the nature thing too. But when do you think clothes became the foundation of our success? Are they really what make us beautiful? If you

24

spend all your time and energy on your exterior, what happens to your real beauty? Let's keep digging and see if we can figure that out.

> Don't be concerned about the outward beauty that depends on fancy hairstyles, expensive jewelry, or beautiful clothes. You should be known for the beauty that comes from within, the unfading beauty of a gentle and quiet spirit, which is so precious to God. That is the way the holy women of old made themselves beautiful.
>
> 1 Peter 3:3–6 NLT

Now I'm not saying to let yourself go and stop bathing, wearing makeup, or shaving. Please don't do that! That would be going from one extreme to another. Don't do it. **God isn't forbidding you to look cute**; he's just asking you not to make that the focus of who you are. Your beauty has more to do with your confidence and faith than it does with what brand of jeans you wear or whether your shoes go perfectly with your outfit.

Justin Note And a here's a hint, girls: **Guys couldn't care less** about that stuff. In fact, they **don't even notice your shoes.** The perfect pair of shoes or matching accessories isn't going to get him. He might not know it, but what he's really looking for is your sparkle. Your charm. Your girly nature. Your spirit. All of that shines brighter than your clothing style and your brand sense. Now like we said in *Dateable*, it's cool to have your own quirky sense of fashion, but you don't have to be a clothes horse to be cool. You just have to be you.

25

Beauty is more about what you know inside of you.
Knowing you are beautiful because of who you are. Knowing
you are fun, loving, lovable, kind, caring, all the good stuff that
you are inside. Beauty comes from deep in your soul. As Brit-
tany Murphy once said, "The sexiest thing on a girl is happiness." Not her outfit. So if you're trying to find your beauty on
the racks at Nordstrom's, know that you'll have to look a long
time, because it isn't there.

Okay, before you close the book for today, look at the verse
from 1 Peter 3 again. **Write it on a 3 x 5 card** or a piece of paper
or in a journal. Then read it out loud 10 times. Put it on your mirror so you can look at it every time you check yourself out. Take
it with you to school. Talk about it with your friends. See what
they think. Start a discussion and see where it leads you. Find out
where beauty really lies and write down the stuff you learn.

Here's where you get your spiritual workout. **This is the
magazine-free zone.** This week don't pick up one single mag.
Don't look over clothing ads in the paper. Don't turn on the
fashion channel. Don't check out who's wearing what in *People*
magazine or on E! Stay away from the fashion police for an
entire week. Let the verse you're learning be your stylist. Let
it wash over you and help you figure out where your beauty
really comes from.

One more thing and you'll be done. Ask yourself these
questions and write down the answers:

6 What makes me unique (i.e., different from other girls)?
my easy-goingness, my loving tender personality
• What makes me funny?
my clutziness, my brain-farts
• What do I do that no one else does?
I don't know

26

- Why do people like me? (If they don't, then write down
    I'm kind, funny, accepting, beautiful, encourager
    why that is. If you think your "not being liked" is a recur-
    ring problem, then you need to start considering ways to
    change that. With an attitude like Christ's, you should be
    very likeable, except to Satan and his minions.)
- How do I make people laugh? *joke about myself*
- How do I care for people? *encourage, pray, listen*
- What have I done for my friends lately? *talked/listened, loved them*
- Why would I want to be friends with me?
    bcuz I make others feel good

If you're like me, your gut instinct is to cringe when you have
to basically compliment yourself, but believe me, it's crucial. You
have to be able to be honest with yourself before you can be
honest with your God. So if you didn't write anything down, go
back, look at these questions and get real with yourself. Don't
hide, don't shut the book, don't lie. Just tell all the good stuff
about yourself and smile. You are good!

27

Girls Don't Fight Other Girls — EVER

by Hayley Morgan

Have you ever noticed how *mean* girls can be? Of course I'm not talking about *you*, just those *other* girls. I mean, those **girls are the most vindictive, backstabbing, harsh creatures on the planet.** They will do whatever it takes to look better than, or at least not worse than, someone else. **But that's not you, right?** You're a nice girl. I mean, you've never trashed one of your friends because they bought the exact same clothes as you. Or gotten totally upset because another girl talked to *your* bf. And **you've never 3-way called** someone to find out what they thought about you. And I'm sure **you never get revenge,** even if it's totally justified. Nope, because you're not mean, but those other girls are just flat-out mean. They seem obsessed with beating other girls to the guy. They have to look better, be better, and feel better than every other girl in class or die trying. So what's the real issue here? Hmmm . . . could it be that all girls are searching for the core answer to the question *Am I beautiful?*

The trouble is that they've started to find the answer to that question by first **finding out if other girls are less beautiful.** And it's become survival of the fittest. **Girl against girl.** Do you think God designed it that way? Do you think that true women of God find pleasure in putting others underneath them?

Check 'em out: Romans 2:1; Romans 12:9–21.

28   who judges condemns self   behave like a Christian

The power and beauty of women comes from their nurturing and loving spirit, not from their warfare and backstabbing. And believe me, girls, guys notice your catfights and they aren't impressed. Women who unite with one another and take care of each other are much more loving and faithful to their God and their people. The point when women started to turn on each other was the point of their destruction. It's like this: If you are calling another girl a dirty name like *slut* or *whore* (or worse), then you are systematically destroying the female species. You aren't just hurting her, you are hurting yourself and all the girls who will come after you. Girls whine about guys messin' up girls' lives, but it's really other girls who do the messin'. We should be encouraging each other to reach for the stars, but instead we spend our time plotting against each other. Strength comes in numbers and support, not in destruction of and hatred for our own sex.

Don't hit back, discover beauty in everyone. If you've got it in you, get along with everybody. Don't insist on getting even; that's not for you to do. "I'll do the judging," says God. "I'll take care of it."

Romans 12:17 MESSAGE

HEAVY Lifting

It's time to get really honest with yourself and with your God. Remember, **"no one is righteous, not even one."** Think back over the past few months. What kinds of names have you called other girls? And don't say "none," because you know that's not true. Get real!

29

What names have you called other girls in the last 2 months?

*not out loud though*

_no_

_b — *_

perfect — envy/jealousy

Have you 3-way called?   Yes   (No)
Have you talked bad about another girl?   (Yes)   No
Gossiped?   (Yes)   No
Got revenge?   Yes   (No)

If you can't be honest here and tell God what you've done, you can't move on in your faith and get closer to him. It's gotta happen.

If we confess our sins, he is faithful and just and will forgive us our sins and purify us from all unrighteousness. If we claim we have not sinned, we make him out to be a liar and his word has no place in our lives.

1 John 1:9–10 NIV

Okay, so here goes. You don't have to write it here, but find someplace to write them out. **All that crappy stuff you've done to other girls. This is your confession.** Make it good.

{ _held grudges, not talked to them, called them names in my head_ }

Did you do it? Don't read on until you've done it. If you were girl enough to do it, then let's go on. You have **two options here:** You can either **read this list to the Father** and trust him for forgiveness, or you can **find someone you really, really**

30

trust who will offer you the forgiveness of Christ. Try a youth pastor or a parent (and not a girl at school who might blab it all). Sometimes this is the best way because we need to hear from another human that what we did was forgiven. It also **adds to the embarrassment factor when you have to confess**, which helps you remember you never want to do that again.

Confess your sins **to each other** and pray for each other so that you may be healed. The earnest prayer of a righteous person has great power and wonderful results.

James 5:16 NLT, emphasis added

Congrats! I'm proud of you for coming clean with your junk. And **God is happy with you too.** Listen, you aren't a bad girl because you slammed other girls; you're just a bad girl if you *keep* on slamming 'em. **You have a clean slate now.** Your beauty is becoming more and more powerful with every step you take toward Christ.

31

Believe in YOUR BEAUTY
by Hayley Morgan

Here's the story, the Fairy Tale Gone Bad:

> **Once upon a time, a girl was born beautiful.** But as she grew up, things happened. **People did or said things to crush her image,** which made her believe that she was no longer good enough, that she was not the beauty that guys desired, and that she was ugly, stupid, and undesirable. As she grew she knew she was plain. She didn't believe compliments she received. She felt like they just couldn't be true. She called herself fat. She dreamed of being a beauty but knew it would never happen to the likes of her. She tried new outfits, new exercises, and new angles but never felt the beauty that was there when she was a little girl.

Every girl has at least one of those crushing moments, that first time when she realized that she wasn't good enough. Think back. Go through the history channel of your life. **Remember the specific point when you first figured out you weren't beautiful?** It might have been something your dad said or didn't do. It might have been something another girl said when she was teasing you. It might have been the first day you got a zit. Just think back. Do you remember the first time you ever felt ugly?

See, **it's a great plan of God's enemy to convince God's beautiful creation that she isn't beautiful at all.** Then he can play on her natural instinct to *be* beautiful by convincing her that there are people besides God who can *make* her beautiful. If

32

you are really made in God's image, then you must have been made right—no broken parts, nothing falling off, nothing too small, too big, or too round. You were perfect at one time. When did it all go downhill? When did you buy the lie? When did beauty become defined as "anything but you"?

Think about it. **When was the first time you realized you had to work at beauty?** When was the first time the pure you wasn't enough? Remember? It will probably be the first thing you think of, since your subconscious remembers it oh-so-well. Take a tour of your past and find that defining moment. *Jesse? 8th grade? 5 6th grade?*

Got it? Okay. Now I believe that at that point in time **your beauty began to be covered up.** Notice I didn't say "taken away," 'cuz it can't be, but it sure can be covered up so that you forget it's even there. That first time someone covered up your beauty with ugliness, that moment in time when the little girl lost her innocence, **that is your beauty's defining moment, so we are going to redefine it.** Yep, we are going to take away the bad that someone did to you or that you imagined on your-self and replace it with a new, more honest defining moment. See, whatever happened eons ago has no real bearing on who you really are and how beautiful you become. You only think it does, or your subconscious thinks it does. See, **your brain is kinda like a dog.** It only believes what you tell it. That's why brainwashing works so well. Sit. Lie down. You are getting very, very sleepy. When people hear things over and over, they start to believe it, and sometimes it only takes one traumatic event to reprogram a lifetime of thought. Check out Romans 12:2 and **write it down here.**

v.1 I beseech you therefore, brethren, by the mercies of God, that you present your bodies a living sacrifice, holy, acceptable to God, which is your reasonable service.

v.2 And don't be conformed to this world, but be transformed by the renewing of your mind, that you may prove what is that good and acceptable and perfect will of God.

33

This is what we are going to do today—reprogram (renew) your mind. So hold on to your gray matter, 'cuz here we go.

Okay, go **someplace where you can be alone.** Take your **Bible** and a **pencil.** Go to your room, a basement, anywhere no one will bother you for **at least 20 minutes.** Make sure you are comfortable and the room is quiet. Now what you are going to do is **remember the event that stole your beauty,** or rather covered it up. You are going to remember where you were, how it smelled that day, what the weather was, all the details exactly as they were, with one exception. Someone will be there whom you didn't notice before. He's going to be standing right beside you, holding your hand. It's **Jesus. He's going back in time with you to fix that fateful day.**

Before you close your eyes to remember, open your Bible and **write down a few verses about the character of Jesus and the confidence he gives you.** It will help to think on these before you imagine him.

Isaiah 54:17 – No one can whip you _No weapon formed against you shall prosper_

Luke 17:6 – You can do anything _Lord said, "If you have faith of a mustard seed, you can say to this tree, Be pulled up by the roots and be planted in the sea' and it would obey you."_

Hebrews 4:16 – Be bold _Let us therefore come boldly to the throne of grace, that we may obtain mercy and find grace to help in time of need._

Matthew 28:18 – He has complete authority _And Jesus came and said, "All authority has been given to me in heaven and on earth."_

John 16:33 – He kicked butt _These things I have spoken to you, that in Me you may have peace; In the world you will have tribulation; but be of good cheer, I have overcome the world._

34

The Ripple-Effect Life

2 Timothy 1:7 – You got the power _For God has not given us a spirit of fear, but of power and of love and of a sound mind._

Whatever memory you want to reprogram, **go back to it now.** After you read this paragraph, **close your eyes** and see it all there in front of you and **Jesus beside you.** Hear what was said to you, and then **listen to Jesus** and hear what he wants to tell you. Let him be his own forgiving, loving, good self. Let him protect you and take you from that bad place. **Let him tell you that you are beautiful.** Let him walk you outside into the sunlight. Let him dance with you. Whatever it might be that he wants to do, let him. This is a form of prayer that will heal the past memory and bring Jesus into that part of your life. So go ahead, give it a shot. Close 'em!

If this seems too wacked to you, that's cool. But check it out; it's totally scriptural. Write down Philippians 4:8 here:

Whatever things are true whatever things are noble, whatever things are just, whatever things are pure, whatever things are lovely, whatever things are of good report, if there is any virtue and if there is anything praiseworthy — Meditate on these things.

What does it tell you to do? Just to make sure that it's coming through loud and clear, I've got a quiz for ya:

Quiz: Philippians 4:8

1. I am supposed to control my thoughts. (T) F
2. I have the ability to become happy by thinking good stuff. (T) F
3. God wants me to think only true and good stuff. (T) F

35

2 Peter 2:19 NLT

4. It isn't what happens to me but what I *think* about what happens to me that matters. (T) F

5. Bad memories make for bad feelings, and God isn't about bad. (T) F

6. God hates it when I lie to myself. (T) F

Scoring: *Give yourself one point for every True you circled and two points for every False you circled. Then add 'em up.*

5–6: Little Miss Thang! *Way to go. You're getting it. God wants you to be in control of your thoughts. 'Cuz if you aren't, then who the heck is?*

7–8: Mind over matter. *You are so close yet so far. You're almost there; you just need to start telling yourself the truth **all** of the time, not just when it's convenient.*

9–12: Dang, girl! *What's up with you? Do you think that someone else can take better control of your life than you can? Go back and check out these verses. Write 'em down. Memorize 'em. Meditate on 'em. Do whatever it takes to get your brain to kick into the fact that God wants you to get control of it. Here they are: Romans 12:2; James 3:2; 4:7; 2 Peter 2:19.*

You are a slave to whatever controls you.

36

Date Night—it isn't what you think. It isn't about hooking up or making out; it's about a night to get together with your crush or your group to do something different. It's not a sexual thing or even a romantic thing; **it's an adventure thing.** On Date Night you are going to **push your limits.** You are going to **think about things you've never thought about before** and **do things you've never done before**. You are going to **get out of the house** and maybe even out of the neighborhood. You are going to **find out things about yourself** and about your crush or friends. So don't get the wrong idea, your Date Night is going to be **a dare night.** Dare yourself to get out of your comfort zone and get involved in the circle of life (sorry, bad *Lion King* reference).

Okay, here's the plan for your first Date Night. Do this on whatever night of the week you want to. If you're following the "How to Use This Book" steps, you'll do it on Friday, but hey, you're big kids now, so you can do it whenever you want. Your choice, but our rules.

CITY BUS

The city bus. You've seen it. You've heard it. And you've most definitely smelled it. It's the blood vessel of the city, carrying all the workers to their jobs and all the shoppers to their stores. It's sometimes filthy, sometimes loud, and sometimes lonely. The people who ride it don't seem to have a lot of energy. They aren't all smiles, and they definitely aren't social. Until today.

37

Your mission, should you choose to accept it, is to buy a ticket for the city bus. Don't know how? Good, that's part of the adventure. Figure it out. Buy your ticket and board the bus. **You have one goal: to make people feel like someone cares about them.** Many of the people you will find on the bus will be empty inside. And lots will be angry. So don't play the freak. Don't cross into their personal space, push yourself on them, or try to make them hug you. But do try to **do stuff that you think might make a stranger's day.** Pay the fare for the working woman who is getting on in a hurry. Carry the bags for the old lady you see standing on the street corner waiting to get on. Tell the girl sitting next to you that you like her coat. Make small talk that makes people feel good.

You are Christ's hand on their lives. If you want to pray for them, try this. Sit in the back of the bus and **imagine Jesus getting on the bus.** Imagine him walking down the aisle and sitting by someone. What would he say to them? Imagine it. How would he interact with people? Imagine it. This is your prayer, your imagined prayer. God knows your thoughts before they are words, so this is your way of asking his blessing on the lives of people. Get to know the outgoing ones. Offer to help the weak ones. Enjoy life! Enjoy God's creation. And enjoy one another.

Explore life. Explore your night. And most of all, have a wonderific time.

Location Note: If there aren't any bus routes near you, drive over to the nearest big city. And if that's just too dang far, then figure out some other way to do things like this for people. Meet people at Wal-Mart, pump gas, or go to a busy neighborhood. Be creative.

Stupidity Prevention Note: Now don't be a fool and go into some dangerous neighborhood you've never been to before, and

38

if you're 14, don't just go jump on a bus and get your parents all freaked out. You and your crush or your group should do this together. If your group is big, split up into groups of 4. Be safe. Be smart. Talk it over with your fam, your youth pastor, whoever. Let someone know where you're going. But be daring and try a new route, one you've never taken.

Road Trip wrap-up

When you are done, get back together and chat about your night:

What happened?

How did it feel?

Who did you meet?

Why did you do what you did?

What did Jesus think of it all?

Was your prayer effective?

NOTES

_____

_____

_____

_____

_____

_____

_____

39

FOCUS GROUP

1. He Said, She Said Improv – guys play girls and girls play guys
2. Show-and-Tell – what did you do, learn, see all week?
3. Q&A – each side asks 5 questions

1. Group Activity—He Said, She Said Improv

If you are doing this book in a group, get ready for a switcheroo. This week you get to show the guys what you really think of them by playing them. Check it out. (If you are doing this with just your crush, then you can skip to the next section, Show-and-Tell.)

Sick of the stupid things guys say and do? Now's the time to show 'em. Today you get to be a guy. Don't get used to it, though; it's only for 20 minutes. Then back to girlsville. We've listed three scenarios there. You'll need thespian volunteers, 4 girls and 4 guys. In these sketches the girls act out the guys' part and the guys are the girls. You can use props, hats, wigs, dresses, whatever. Each improv should be 3 to 5 minutes long with 2 to 4 people involved. Have fun!

The Big Date (2 girls, 2 guys) – The guy (played by the girl) has to pick up the girl (played by the guy) for a date. Meet the parents. Drive to the restaurant. Order dinner, eat, and then go home.

The Crush (2 guys, 2 girls) – In 2 groups of friends, the girls and the guys like each other but are afraid to say so. They go out together. How do they all act around each other? (Remember, girls play the guys and guys play the girls.)

The Breakup (1 or 2 guy, 1 or 2 girls) – The guy (played by the girl) wants to break up with the girl (played by the guy). How will he do it? How will she react? Friends can be involved if you want.

Note: These are just ideas to get you started. You can change 'em up however you want. You are the *artiste (say this in French, it sounds better).*

40

2. Show-and-Tell

We'll get to the Q&A soon, but before you start the interrogations, give each other a leg up and tell the guys what your week was about. Give them the highlights of what you learned, did, and experienced. They did different stuff than you, so fill 'em in so you are all on equal ground. Take 5 minutes to show and tell.

3. Q&A

Okay, now you can start the games! This is the same drill as the kickoff: **5 questions for the girls, 5 questions for the guys, 5 minutes to answer each one.** Ask away. Here are some discussion questions to get you started, or you can make them up on your own. Asking this kind of girl Qs will help you get to the bottom of the male psyche. But make up your own too. Have fun.

- What (besides the obvious physical stuff) do you like about girls 'cuz it is so girly and so good?
- What lies do you hear girls telling themselves and each other?
- What do you think it means to be a man?
- What besides the physical stuff makes a girl beautiful? What makes a girl ugly?
- Do you like it when a girl asks you out? Why?
- Do you like it when a girl is mysterious? Why?
- Do you prefer talking or listening? shopping or hunting? adventure or safety? getting over it or getting even?

These might not be questions you like, so come up with your own. We just wanted to get the juices flowing.

41

Week

two

Mystery Girl

And this is his command: to **believe** in the name of his Son, Jesus Christ, **and** to **love** one another as he commanded us.

1 John 3:23 NIV

"Love the Lord your God with all your heart and with all your soul and with all your mind and with all your strength." . . . "Love your neighbor as yourself." There is no commandment greater than these.

Mark 12:30–31 NIV

You can read it like this or go it alone.
Read it however you want to this week.

How to Read This Book This Week		
Monday	read 'Be MysTerious' and 'AcT ConfidenT'
Tuesday	read 'Look 'Em in The Eye'
Wednesday	Take The nighT off
Thursday	read 'ShuT Your MouTh'
Friday	DaTe NighT
Saturday	Take The day off
Sunday	Focus Group

Be mysterious

by Hayley Morgan

Okay, I hate to admit it, but I watch all those **bachelor and dating shows.** You know the ones where the guy goes out with like 26 women until he narrows it down to 4, then 2, then 1 lucky girl who gets to marry her dream man? Those ones. Yep, I watch 'em. I watch 'em, and I laugh. But I also take notes, 'cuz you can really learn a lot about human nature from those things. Like one major thing I've noticed, and maybe you have too: **It seems like the girl that all of the guys pick isn't the sweetest one, or the hottest one, or even the best one, but it's the most mysterious one.** He always says something like, "She hasn't opened up to me as much as the other girls. There's just some kind of mystery to her, something I can't figure out and I'd just love to explore further." I promise you that the guy has said it on every show. It's frustrating to the rest of the girls. They say stuff like, "I don't see why he likes *her*. She's not really into him like some of us are. I mean, I'm totally ready to share my whole life with him, and she just seems not as interested." And every time they say that, I stand up and scream at the TV, "Duh! That's *exactly* why he's into her! Because **she hasn't dumped all her feelings on him like you have!** She hasn't asked him to 'define the relationship' and crap like that."

Understand one thing. **If you want to be the prize all the guys are after, then shut up and be mysterious.** This was a major chapter in *Dateable,* and if you already read it, then you get the concept but maybe not the how-tos. Good thing you picked up this book, 'cuz here we go.

Guys are hunters, they are competitors, **they love a challenge,** and that's why they go for the mysterious girl. They want

44

the girl who doesn't "tell all." They want the one who isn't all emotional and overbearing. They want the one they aren't sure they can really get. It's like Woody Allen, the old actor/director guy, once said: "I wouldn't want to be a member of any club that would want me as a member." It's a guy's nature to want whatever or whoever is the hardest thing to get. So this chapter is going to teach you how to be that mystery girl that all the guys are drawn to. I'm going to divulge the intimate secrets of the guy's mind so you can finally figure out what a guy wants. So are ya ready?

Before we go too far, you need to be totally honest with yourself, and this quick quiz can help. Get a pencil and do it right now. It isn't that hard!

Quiz: How Mysterious are you?

1. When I talk on the phone with my crush, I:
   a. tell everything I did all day, all the gory details, 'cuz it bonds us
   b. just listen, 'cuz he really likes to tell me about his day
   c. like to make him laugh. I don't get too serious or mushy

2. When I am mad at my girlfriend, I:
   a. tell my mom all about it
   b. tell my crush all about it
   c. tell the whole school about it
   d. all of the above

3. Whenever I go out with a guy, I:
   a. always, always pay. I'm all for equal rights
   b. ask him if I can help with the check
   c. let him pay, 'cuz he asked me out

4. When it comes to other girls and my crush, I:
   a. get totally jealous. I mean, he's *my* crush!
   b. other girls? Who cares? He likes me
   c. make sure to tell her he's already taken

45

5. When stuff really sucks, I:
   a. talk about it with other people. Some might say it's complaining, but hey, if something's bad, somebody better say something
   b. just suck it up; life is too short
   c. walk away. I'd rather forget about it than have to do something that's so totally stupid

Scoring:

1. a = 3, b= 2, c = 1

2. a = 1, b = 3, c = 3, d = 3

3. a = 3, b= 2, c = 1

4. a = 3, b = 1, c = 2

5. a = 3, b = 1, c = 2

5: Mystery Queen. *You must be a guy magnet. It looks like you really are a charming, God-centered girl who hasn't made guys her all and all. Congrats!*

6–11: Find a key and lock your lips. *You're blabbin' way too much. Remember how much fun it was to search for the hidden Easter eggs? Don't put all the eggs on the table and tell him, "Here they are." Give him a chance to hunt.*

12–15: Open book. *I bet people run when they see you coming. Too much information too soon. Try holding it in a little bit. Don't give us all the info all the time—you aren't CNN.*

More than looks, more than body, more than beauty, more than anything, a guy is drawn to mystery. It must be tied back to his relationship to his Creator. If God isn't a mystery, then who is? I tell you straight up, there's nothing more alluring to a guy than a woman who understands the power of mystery and uses it. Now, station break real quick: I'm **not talking about some kind of spy novel thriller chick who dresses in all black** and breaks into people's houses to steal diamonds.

46

Although to some guys that's somewhat exciting, it's not really the point of all this. Let me break it down.

I think there are **8 little words that define a girl of mystery**. These 8 words become her mantra. She says them every day. She believes them. She shapes her life around them. And most of all she lives them. Check it out:

> Be still, and know that I am God.
>
> Psalm 46:10 NIV

Imagine a girl who really lives this verse.

Okay, don't mind if I do. This is how she looks to all the guys as she walks by: **calm (still), cool (knows who's God), and collected (and it shows).** She doesn't need to talk about other girls or look down on them, because she trusts her God with her life. She cares about other people. **She laughs. She jokes.** She saves her emotional breakdowns for her girlfriends who can handle them and not her guy friends who are clueless. She understands how much information people can handle and only gives them that much. She is charming. She is mysterious, and every guy wants to know what makes her so confident.

Now don't freak out if you aren't all that mysterious, 'cuz we're gonna give you the mystery recipe that will produce by far the most mysterious woman on campus. So you ready for the next chapter?

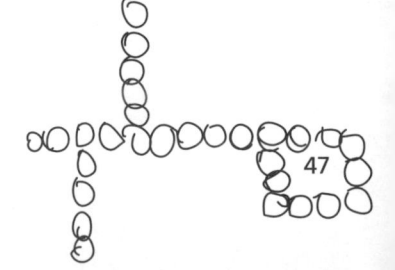

47

ACT CONFIDENT

by Hayley Morgan

onfidence is the key ingredient when creating a mystery girl. It's essential. It's the flour to your cake; it's the meat to your meat loaf. Essential. I'm telling you, it's easy for a girl with confidence to be a total mystery to a guy. But I can hear you screaming again, "Confidence? I don't have any freakin' confidence! Where do I get *that*?" Well, I'm glad you asked. Walk into my confidence store and follow me to the dressing room. Have a seat on the soft velvet chair by the wall and listen. Confidence is a state of mind, not a reality. That means **you don't have to *be* confident to *act* confident.** You following me?

It's like this: Nobody knows what goes on inside your head except you and God. All anybody else knows is what you *say* and what you *do*. So if I were to teach you what a confident girl says and does, you too could look like a confident girl. Make sense?

Let's say you are going to a party and you are scared to death. You are shy. You don't like talking to people, and besides, you hardly know anyone. What will you do? Here, try on this great little outfit from the racks here at the confidence store. Slip it on over your head, slide into it, and feel the comfort. **You're "Confidence Girl" now, so this is what you do.** At home before the party, you dress in whatever makes you feel most attractive. Your favorite sweater, your best jeans, whatever makes you think you look good. Then when you get to the party, you walk in with your **head up, breathing** (you always remember to breathe), **with a real smile, not a fake one.** You look people in the eye and care about them in one glance.

48

Confidence is a state of mind,

You're **nice to everyone.** You walk through the crowd saying "excuse me" in the nicest voice anyone's ever heard. When you get to the food table, you ask the first person you see how they are doing. When you ask the person how they are, you look them in

A girl with confidence always cares more about how other people are doing than about herself.

the eye and wait to hear what they say. You actually care what their answer is. You might comment on someone else's nice shirt or cool haircut. Remember, **you live to make other people feel good.** The secret is that you know deep down that everyone is as scared as you are and that your God has filled you with enough love to help them all feel better.

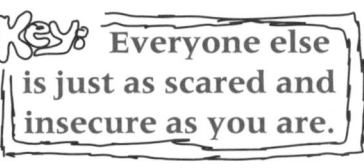

Everyone else is just as scared and insecure as you are.

Confidence Girl is not afraid to laugh at herself. When you almost trip and fall on your way to the couch, you say something like, "Have that removed" and laugh with everyone else as you walk on. **When you laugh off your mistakes, you're charming.** People become drawn to you. Now you don't slam yourself, because you're too proud of who you are as a child of God to slam his creation, but you aren't afraid to laugh at your screwups.

Yeah, Confidence Girl is attractive. In fact, you're attractive not only to guys but to other girls too—that means that girls like you. You're just a really nice person, hard to hate and great to be around. And the

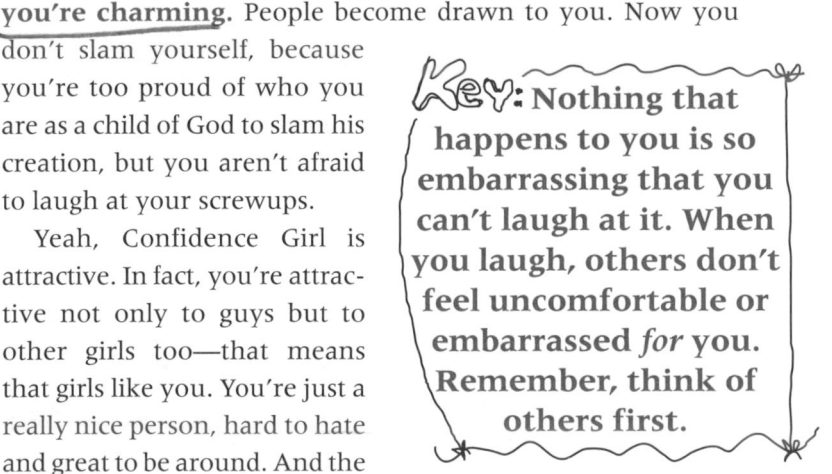

Key: Nothing that happens to you is so embarrassing that you can't laugh at it. When you laugh, others don't feel uncomfortable or embarrassed *for* you. Remember, think of others first.

49

not a reality.

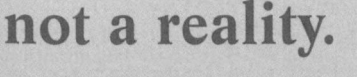

coolest part is that God taught you all this stuff. It's all an exercise in being "holy as I am holy" (1 Peter 1:16).

Confidence Girl has these verses graffitied all over her heart, and she knows how to use 'em. She lives to serve God and others, not herself. Not her ego, not her hurt feelings, and not her pride. And because of that, she is the queen of confidence.

Serving others = Confidence

Mark 9:35 NIV	If anyone wants to be **first**, he **must be the very last**. . . .
Romans 15:8 NIV	For I tell you that **Christ has become a servant**. . . .
1 Corinthians 9:19–22 AMP	. . . **I have made myself a bond servant to everyone, so that I might gain the more** . . . .
Mark 10:45 NIV	For even the Son of Man **did not come to be served, but to serve**. . . .
1 Corinthians 6:7–8 NIV	**Why not rather be wronged?** . . .
2 Corinthians 11:30 NIV	If I must boast, I will boast of the things that show my **weakness**.
Galatians 5:6 NIV	The **only thing that counts** is faith expressing itself through **love**.
Galatians 5:26 NIV	Let us **not** become **conceited**, provoking and envying each other.
Galatians 6:4–5 NIV	Each one should test his own actions. Then he can take pride in himself, **without comparing himself** to somebody else. . . .

See, **confidence isn't about being all cocky and self-assured; it's about being all holy and giving a rip about other people.** That's one of the reasons it's so dang attractive. It's that part of Christ in you that is so amazing.

If people are laughing at you,

Let's do a **quick study on Christ.** He is our model. He's the one we are supposed to be like. Open up your Bible and find these verses: Ephesians 5:2; Isaiah 53:7; Romans 15:8. Jot down a few notes, a few key words that would describe Jesus based on these verses.

> Eph. 5:2 ~ walk in love as Jesus loved us and gave himself for us
>
> Is. 53:7 ~ Jesus was oppressed, but did not open his mouth.
>
> Rom 15:8 ~ Jesus became a servant

Now let's just **check his confidence factor.**

Answer these questions about Jesus. If you have to, look it up in a concordance or something, but find verses that help you understand his confidence.

Did Jesus worry about what other people thought of him? *No*
Did he care about everyone he met? *Yes*
Did he think more about others than himself? *Yes*
Did he gossip? *No*
Did he cut people down because they made him look bad? *No*
Do you think he got mad when he slipped and fell on the
  hard ground and the disciples started to laugh? *No*
Did he look people in the eye when he met them? *Yes*
Do you think he smiled a lot? *Yes*

Jesus *was* confidence. Check him out in some more verses: Matthew 26:51–54; Luke 6:27–28; 9:23–24; John 11:41; 16:33.
Jesus fulfilled scripture   love enemies   take up your cross JC thanks God   JC has overcome world

If your goal as a believer is to become more like JC, then now you know where you are going. He was a confident human being, one who cared more for others than himself. In every relationship you have, consider how Jesus would love the person, no matter how insecure you might feel. HWJL? Give love and get love.

it's 'cuz you're not laughing.

51

Look 'em in the Eye

by Hayley Morgan

So the best and most beautiful thing about a mystery girl is her confidence. But what does this mean in a relationship with a guy? Let's just give you an overview, shall we?

If the Bible's true and Jesus *is* in your body—**"you are in me, and I am in you"** (John 14:20)—then you have it in you to be just as confident as he was. A mystery girl doesn't date a guy to make her look good or feel better. She has her own friends and doesn't dump them when she hooks up with someone. She doesn't dump all her problems on a guy; she saves that for God and girls. (Girls bond by dumping on each other. Guys don't.) And she isn't always available. She's busy. She's got stuff. She believes in who she is and it shows. She doesn't have to cut other girls down to feel better; in fact, she wants to build them up to feel better. She won't gossip; it's too unholy. And she would never, ever, ever, ever do a 3-way call to figure out what someone thought about her. Remember, "be still, and know that I am God."

So **here's what you do when you don't feel confident:**

Step 1: Psalm 46:10 *ซู be still and know that I am God.*

Step 2: Shut up

Step 3: Smile

Step 4: Laugh

Step 5: Remember who you are. The child of a king. The heiress to the kingdom. You are royalty, little girl, so act like it!

52

Lots of people seem to think that you win friends and influence people by controlling and manipulating them. But the truth of the matter is, **you become a huge influencer of people, maybe even a generation, and have hundreds of friends when you stop looking out for number one and start caring about others—that's confidence.**

"If anyone wants to be **first**, he **must be the very last**, and the servant of all" (Mark 9:35).

=HEAVY LIFTING=

Okay, so I've beat confidence to the ground, but you've got to get it. It will literally change your life. Now it's time to practice it. So here's the deal: Sometime in the next week I want you to walk into a room where you don't know many people, or at least don't usually talk to many people, and **practice your confidence.**

Walk in with your shoulders back, eyes wide open, and a real smile goin'. Walk up to someone and say "How are you doing?" And then stop and listen to them. Find someone interesting, someone you don't usually talk to, and make conversation. I can hear you now—"But I don't know what to say. I'm too shy. Blah, blah, blah, blah!" Shut up. You are *not* too shy. And I'll *give* you things to say. If you claim to be a Christian and you say you love God, then guess what's next? Love your neighbor as yourself. I'm teaching you how to do that. So calm down. Focus. And get ready to begin the adventure of being a major tool in God's hands.

Here's some things you can say. Change 'em up to fit the sitch. Use your brain; it's part of your beauty.

Key: When in doubt, compliment, but mean it.

53

Weather:

> "Man, it's really been hot, huh?"
>
> "The rain always makes me want to take a nap."
>
> "Did you see that lightning last night?"
>
> (or just improvise something else)

Clothes:

> "I love those jeans. Where did you get them?"
>
> "I have that same T-shirt. Don't you just love it?"
>
> "What a cool belt."

Classes:

> "Did you get that social studies homework? Weird, huh?"
>
> "So what college are you thinking of going to?"
>
> "Aren't you in my bio class? Do you get biology? It's way hard for me."

> **KEY:**
> **People love to talk about themselves, so give them the opportunity to do that.**

Friends/Family:

> "Was that your sister out there on the track earlier?"
>
> "Where do you guys live?"
>
> "Doesn't your dad work at Macy's?"

> **KEY:**
> **Don't brag. It isn't cute.**

So you've got your homework. Good luck! I know you can do it 'cuz I've got confidence in you.

A girl with confidence always looks people in the

eye.

SHUT YOUR MOUTH
by Hayley Morgan

Okay, you got your confidence on. Getting out in the mix. You are out-complimenting your friends and, even more importantly, out-accepting their compliments. Now check out this girl.

Chastity is a whiner. She doesn't think so, of course, but she complains about everything. "I don't whine, I just point out where stuff is wrong," she says. You just know that if something doesn't go her way, she's gonna tell you about it. It's just part of her nature. She's **a talker**. She loves to talk. **Complain, talk, gab,** whatever, just let her talk. The best part of her day is when she can talk about someone else. "Can you believe Melissa?" "Did you hear about Jack?" It makes her feel good down to her core to tell people what she knows about other people. She feels a sense of power in the knowing.

And if any girl even thinks about talking to her boyfriend, look out. Catfight. She's all over her. I mean, a girl's gotta protect her territory, right? Yeah, Chastity is an interesting girl. But here's my question: Is she a good girl? Is she one that every guy runs out to catch? Is she a fun friend? Is she an example of holiness, or of selfishness?

In case you were too sleepy to notice, **I just described most of the girls in your class.** Face it, it's true, **girls' faults are really obvious, and they all start with the mouth.** You know the scene, girl against girl. Power struggle of the mouth. Who can talk the most smack? Who can make the best show? **The mouth is the power tool of choice for girls.**

People can tame all kinds of animals and birds and reptiles and fish, but no one can tame the tongue. It is an uncontrollable evil, full of deadly poison. Sometimes it praises our

56

Lord and Father, and sometimes it breaks out into curses against those who have been made in the image of God. And so blessing and cursing come pouring out of the same mouth. Surely, my brothers and sisters, this is not right! Does a spring of water bubble out with both fresh water and bitter water? Can you pick olives from a fig tree or figs from a grapevine? No, and you can't draw fresh water from a salty pool.

James 3:7–12 NLT

The trouble with the tongue is that it's like trying to build a house using nothing but a chain saw. Makes it kinda hard to put the thing together. It can tear anything apart, but building stuff, that's another matter.

A truly beautiful and confident girl gives her tongue a rest. That means she shuts up! Nothing is more unattractive to a guy than a girl who is slamming another girl.

Can you see Jesus sitting around with Mary and Martha and talking about the other women in the village? "I know, I mean what *was* she thinking when she got dressed this morning? Her sandals don't match her belt!" Can you see Jesus talking

Justin Note: We can tell how nice girls are by how they treat other girls. If you are one of those girls who doesn't get along with any girls, that puts up a red flag—"What's wrong with her that makes her hard to get along with?" Girls can be catty, but the girl who gets my attention is the one who isn't catty back because she's too confident to bother with that kind of junk.

57

mystery girl • week two • mystery girl • week two • mystery girl • week two • mystery girl • week two • mystery girl • wee

⦚⦚⦚ The mouth is the power tool

smack about people behind their backs? Just doesn't compute, does it?

Gossip feels really good, but it's oh-so-bad (Prov. 18:8). The writer of Proverbs talks about it like a good piece of meat. But I like to think about it like an amazing piece of chocolate cake.

Chocolate Cake	Gossip
It's sitting on the table when you walk by.	She looks so bad.
You love chocolate.	It would be so easy to say something funny.
The smell is calling your name.	Your friends are on the same page.
You stop. Your mouth starts to water.	You look at your friends, who giggle, and you start to formulate your words.
You have to have it. It's right there. It's so wonderful and so easy to take, and there's even a fork right next to it. You grab it and dive in. Ecstasy!	"Where does she shop? Animals 'R Us?" Laughter. Ah, such a feeling of ecstasy!

Gossip and slamming others tastes as good to me as chocolate cake. I admit it. I love it. I'm an addict. The hardest thing in the world is when one of my friends says, "I'm not supposed to say anything, but I have to tell somebody." Oh, I so want to know what she has to say. I so want to be in on the juice. "I'm just an innocent listener," I tell myself. "I mean, *she's* the one talking. What can it hurt? And besides, it makes us feel closer. We need this." And blam, there I am listening in on the private life of a friend of a friend. Oh, the guilt, the pain when it's over . . . but boy was it good going down.

58

# of choice for girls.

It's just like the cake. It feels so good in my mouth. And for 2 minutes it's the best part of my day. But 30 minutes later, when I'm coming down off my sugar high and dropping fast, the pain pounds in my head as I realize that I have no self control. Ugh!

Addiction. It isn't just for drugs. **As a girl it's much easier to be addicted to information than to cocaine.** But if you're addicted to words, you are just as bad as the crackhead in the alley—maybe worse, 'cuz your drug is the emotions and lives of others. Ouch! What an ugly thing to feed off of. So what's the answer? How does a girl who loves to talk learn not to eat up all the gossip that she sees? Just like an alcoholic learns to stop drinking. Alcoholics know that they have a problem, so they don't let themselves go places where the problem can get out of hand—i.e., bars. Alcoholics know not to go to bars 'cuz bars have alcohol and alcohol is bad. And girls know not to stay around gossips 'cuz gossips have gossip and gossip is bad. The best thing to do is to tell your friends that you have a real problem with gossip so you just have to remove yourself from it. Each time they start to lay some "news" on you, tell them that. It isn't blaming them, so they won't take it as an insult. And, bonus, it might even get them to thinking about what they let come out of *their* mouths. A girl who doesn't want anything to do with gossip stays away from gossips. If you are at risk, avoid tongues that talk too much. It's your only option for safety.

look them up!

The Proverbial Tongue:

Proverbs

15:28; mouth of wicked speaks evil

17:28; the wise hold their peace

18:8; tattletale's words taste good

18:21; death + life are in the tongue

25:23. backbiting brings anger

59

• mystery girl • week two • mystery girl • week two • mystery girl • week two • mystery girl • week two • mystery girl • w

Heavy Lifting

Shut up. This week you are going to shut up, literally. Pick one day when you vow not to talk. This is going to be a trip, trust me. You won't believe how hard it is, but when you're done you won't believe how you will think before you talk from then on. Before you do this, make sure everyone knows. Tell your fam, your friends, your dog. Let everyone know that mum's the word for one entire day. Weekend, of course. You can't do this during school; you'd get detention. So pick a Saturday that you don't have to work or be anywhere where people will expect you to talk. Take a pad and pencil with you wherever you go so you can communicate when you need to. Don't talk to yourself, the dog, the cat, the guy in the next car. Shut up and listen. Listen to what God is saying. Listen to the wind. Listen to the birds. Listen to the rain. Just listen. Shut up and listen. This might be the hardest thing you ever do, and you might not be girl enough to do it. But if you think you are, then go for it. You will be amazed at the results.

Dorkette Note: Don't just use this as an opp to veg out in front of the TV. Live. Don't just sit and watch life; the silent treatment won't work with a TV in your face. You need to be able to hear God. Take your journal with you someplace. Write about what it feels like. Document the experiment. It'll be a trip.

DATE Night Mystery Date

Well, it's that time again. Time to practice what we've been preaching. No more boring dates—*Dateable Rules* to the rescue! On this Date Night it's all up to the guys. Just wait for them to call, wait for them to plan, and wait for them to take care of you. All you have to do is be nice, conversational, and complimentary.

Yep, there they are again. Compliments. Everyone loves to hear about what a good job they've done. Especially guys. Here's a little note on how a guy likes to be complimented. First, understand girls. Girls love to be complimented on themselves: "I love your hair." "You're the sweetest girl I know." "You have the best taste of anyone I know." But guys are a little different. They prefer to be complimented on what they have *done*. "I love the movie you picked." "This was the most creative date I've been on." "That touchdown was incredible." Compliment what **he did,** not **him.** Make sense? Try it out on this Date Night: "I love this activity." "What a great idea for a date." Stuff like that. Soon you'll have him feelin' so good he'll feel like he's died and gone to heaven.

So let's recap: Your job is to wait for him to plan the date. Accept the invite. Smile. Be happy. No complaining. No fighting. Compliments all around. Got it? Have a blast!

61

1. Lovin' Session – compliments for everyone
2. Show-and-Tell – fill the guys in on what you've read
3. Q&A – do your 5 Qs
4. Party Planning – keep the plans forming

So what did you learn this week? Anything? Do you feel like a new woman? Ready to take on the world and be the most *Dateable* chick ever? Good, then off we go to Focus Group wonderland. Yeah, you're going to do the normal focusing. You know, 5 questions for each group, discussion time, yada yada yada. But here's the added bonus. This time you are going to have a **Lovin' Session**.

For this you need to get your group into a big circle. Each person gets a blank piece of 8½ x 11 paper. Everyone has to write their name across the top of their paper and then pass it to the person to their right. That person is going to write a few sentences on your paper and then pass it on to the person on their right, and so on. These sentences will be compliments, things you like about the person whose name is on the paper. Share the love. "I love that you are so funny and cute. You make my day every time I see you. I am a better person because I know you." Stuff like that. This is a Lovin' Session! Build each other up. Encourage people in their gifts and let them know how much you care. At the end of the circle, you will get your own paper back and will be able to bask in the beauty of kind words for as long as you keep that paper.

(**Boyfriend note:** If it's just you and your boyfriend, then you guys should take 5 minutes to write each other a nice note. Be generous with your words. It isn't every day that he gets to hear how great he is.)

62

After you have done your Lovin' Session, it's time to focus. Recap all that you've read for the guys so they know what's going on, and they will do the same for you. Then get to focusing. 5 questions for you and 5 for them. Same drill as before. Come up with your own questions except for one specific question you have to ask the guys. It's to keep them honest. This week they were told to figure out some risks and take them. So be sure one of your 5 questions is, "What risks did you take this week?" Then watch 'em squirm.

Finish the night by working on the *Dateable* Bash—only one more week before blastoff. Will you be ready? Will the party be lame or legendary? It's up to you, so get the Bash on!

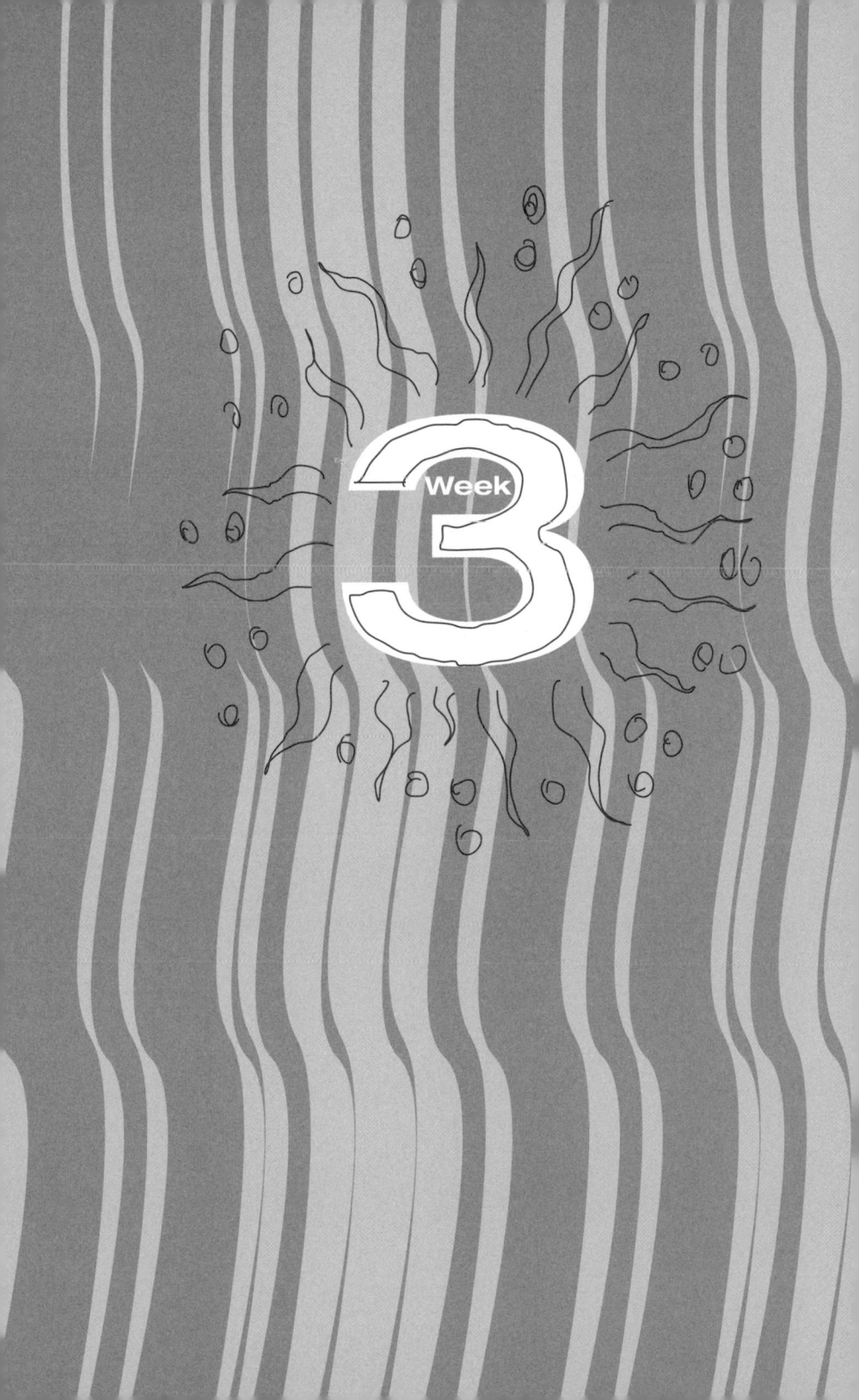

Week

3

Guy power

How to Read This Book This Week	Monday	read "LeT Him Lead"
	Tuesday	Take The day off
	Wednesday	read "Don'T Tell Him Your Life STory"
	Thursday	read "Need Him"
	Friday	read "The DaTe: Who Does WhaT?"
	Saturday	DaTe NighT: Dinner and a Movie
	Sunday	Focus Group

by Hayley Morgan

Finally! We're on the downhill stretch. We've figured out that all this girly stuff is what guys are after. Now it's time to connect the dots between you and him. What can you do to help yourself become the godly, mysterious woman and him become the godly, powerful man?

Let the guy lead! This is the major guy/girl interaction. We talked about this a lot in *Dateable* as well, so let's dive in a bit deeper and see if we can't help you practice it like a pro.

No Shortcuts

Shortcuts are the best. They take the boring factor out of stuff. They get you where you want to go quicker. They're just plain easier. But only when you are driving. If you try shortcuts anywhere else, look out, disaster could be cutting just as short. **A shortcut in life is something we do 'cuz we don't want to pay full price.** We know what we want, but we just aren't willing to wait or just don't trust God for it. That's what you're doing when you're taking shortcuts. It's like this: Either you trust God with your life, or you do everything yourself. And plenty of girls are really into doing it themselves. In fact, it's all the rage. If he won't ask you out fast enough, ask him. If he doesn't call you quick enough, call him. If another girl's scoping him out, protect your territory. Sure, there are all kinds of unspoken "girl rules" these days that totally laugh in the face of God and his timing. **The idea that you have to take your dating life into your own hands is the most ludicrous, insane thing I have ever heard of.** There's 2 things you need to know here:

66

1. You have no control over what other people do, so quit trying to control them.

2. You look like a fool when you take things into your own hands.

I know you aren't thinking about marriage and stuff, but the only info in the Bible about relationships between guys and girls is about marriage and the church. So we will have to use it as a kind of guide. It at least gives us some understanding of what God planned for the two sexes.

> But there is one thing I want you to know: A man is responsible to Christ, a woman is responsible to her husband, and Christ is responsible to God.
>
> 1 Corinthians 11:3 NLT

> As the church submits to Christ, so you wives must submit to your husbands in everything.
>
> Ephesians 5:24 NLT

> Women should listen and learn quietly and submissively. I do not let women teach men or have authority over them. Let them listen quietly.
>
> 1 Timothy 2:11–12 NLT

Now, can you use any of these verses to support you calling him, taking control, or being the leader in the relationship in any way? Let me answer for you: No. You can't. Okay, dig harder. Let's see if you can find any verse anywhere that says anything about women taking the lead in love relationships. We'll make it easy on you. Here are all the New Testament verses about the role of women in guy/girl relationships. Read 'em all. But don't

get too bummed; they don't paint a happy picture of your right to "chase guys."

1 Timothy 2:9–15; 3:11 • Titus 2:3–5 • 1 Peter 3:1–7 • 1 Corinthians 11:11–16 • Colossians 3:18 • Ephesians 5:22–33

Now I'm not trying to fill you full of downers and hand you a knife, but you need to understand that when you take on the role of the guy (asking out, calling, paying, etc.), not only do you mess up your dating relationship but you also mess up your spiritual relationship by telling God you just don't trust him. Don't get caught in the lie. It isn't okay for girls to be guys.

The way I look at it, you have two options. You can either go with the flow of the world and take over where guys have (we'll admit it) fallen miserably short. You can start asking them out, playing the aggressor. Or you can play it by God's rules and "be still and know" that he is God. So which will it be? World's rules or God's rules?

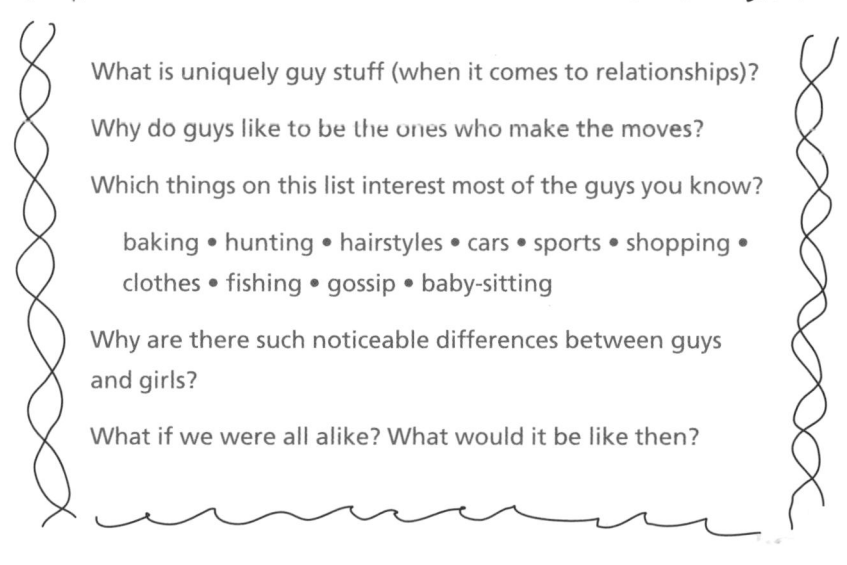

ꙡ ꙡ ꙡ ꙡ ꙡ **Stuff to Ponder** ꙡ ꙡ ꙡ ꙡ ꙡ

What is uniquely guy stuff (when it comes to relationships)?

Why do guys like to be the ones who make the moves?

Which things on this list interest most of the guys you know?

baking • hunting • hairstyles • cars • sports • shopping • clothes • fishing • gossip • baby-sitting

Why are there such noticeable differences between guys and girls?

What if we were all alike? What would it be like then?

68

Don't Tell him your Life story
by Hayley Morgan

irls have done some really stupid stuff in the name of honesty. So let me shed some light on your honesty factor in order to help you be a better girl. Honesty is telling someone the truth. It isn't telling them *everything*. It's like this: If you were married, had 2 little kids and a husband, and just got some major bills in the mail that you couldn't pay, would you get your 5- and 8-year-olds around the table and talk over your poverty with them? Would you tell them that you were worried and you no longer had their lives under control? If you did, you should be shot. But why would it be wrong? It's the truth, isn't it? Yes, but do they need to know it? Does it make their lives better or worse?

Being honest doesn't mean telling people everything that is in your head. That's called dumping, and it really sucks.

Key: The question is always, "Will knowing this make their lives better or worse?" If you can't say "better," then don't say it at all.

The biggest question is, What do they *need* to know? What would make their lives better? And you know what, besides them not *needing* to know all your secrets, you don't *need* to be telling them. See, your life is expressly yours. You have a right to privacy. You have a right to secrets. In fact, you should have some secrets in your life. If you don't, then you're probably not your own person. You probably feel like you need other people's advice or acceptance to be whole. And you need

69

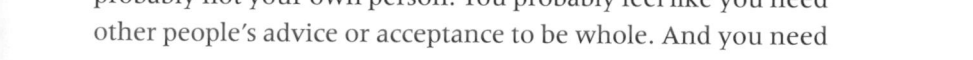

to do a little Bible study to help change your off-balance way of thinking. In fact, a little study time would be good for all of us, so let's dive in again.

Obviously, I'm not trying to be a people pleaser! No, I am trying to please God. If I were still trying to please people, I would not be Christ's servant.

Galatians 1:10 NLT

If you claim to be religious but don't control your tongue, you are just fooling yourself, and your religion is worthless.

James 1:26 NLT

The godly think before speaking; the wicked spout evil words.

Proverbs 15:28 NLT

What goes into a man's mouth does not make him "unclean," but what comes out of his mouth, that is what makes him "unclean."

Matthew 15:11 NIV

All your relationship rules go back to one thing: Love the Lord with all your heart, soul, and strength, and love your neighbor as yourself. In case you still aren't getting it, let me make it clearer. A lot of crappy things have probably happened to you over your lifetime. It feels good to talk them out, and that isn't bad. But always remember that not everyone is ready to hear your problems, and especially not guys. You've had months, even years to work your problems through and think about them, but to others it's all brand-new.

70

Justin Note: Can I just say that as a guy my instinct is to *fix* things? So when you come to me with all your problems, I want more than anything to fix them. But I can't, and that makes me upset. I want to fix things; I need to fix things. So when you dump all this unfixable stuff on me, you overwhelm me, and it's not a good scene.

So don't think that being honest means telling people everything. It doesn't. It only means telling them what will make their lives better. If what you are telling is only to make *your* life better, then that isn't honesty, it's selfishness. And selfishness isn't part of a confident girl.

71

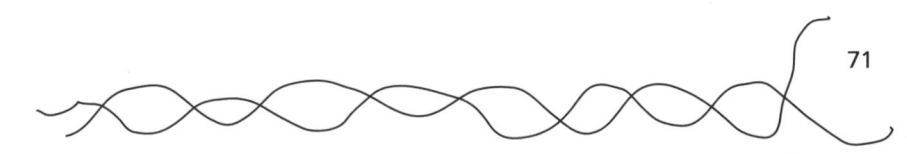

NEED Him

by Hayley Morgan

But in relationships among the Lord's people, women are
not independent of men, and men are not independent
of women.

1 Corinthians 11:11 NLT

Competition is a good thing. It lowers prices; it raises adrenaline.
It's good in a lot of instances, except one. And that is between
guys and girls. Now don't get all huffy. I'm not talking about
a friendly game of touch football or some hoops. I'm talking
about in life. **When girls start taking over the role of guys
and competing to see who's the bigger man, things get
messed up.** If you still aren't tracking with me, let me show
you the life of such a girl.

We'll call her **Melissa.** Melissa is a strong girl. She's confident
in herself. A good student. Great athlete. An all-over solid girl.
She's also totally independent. She can do anything you
can do, only better. She doesn't need a guy to help her carry
her books or to fix her car. She can take care of it all. **She's
her own woman.** She's strong enough to open the door for
herself, thank you very much. She doesn't want guys to think
she's weak and dependent. So she acts strong and independent. Girly stuff grosses her out. You get the picture. Normal,
everyday girl, huh?

But **why isn't she getting any dates?** Hmm. Let's think.
Could it be because she doesn't need any? I mean, what would
a guy do in her life? She's got it all under control. She's doing
everything herself that he would normally like to do for her. So
Melissa has a definite boyfriend void. Sure, she's got lots

72

of guy friends, but it never gets any further than that, and she wonders why.

God didn't make us to be islands, independent women who take care of ourselves. He made us to be interdependent with men. He made it so **our weaknesses are filled by their strengths and vice versa.** The trouble all started back in the '60s with the sexual revolution, when women decided it was just as easy for them to do what the men usually did. And it's true, it is easy. We *can* do it. But we aren't *supposed to.* **As women started taking on more and more male roles, guys started being needed less and less.** And so they lost interest. **Guys need to be needed.** They need a purpose, a function. And a girl like Melissa has factored all of that out of her life. Her independence becomes a deterrent instead of an attractant. It deters guys from offering a helping hand, from getting a door, from being the stronger of the two.

Justin Note: It's true, I need to be needed. I'm man enough to say it. But when you never ever need me, you take away all your beauty. If you don't let me do all the little things 'cuz I'm the man, then I know you won't need me on the big stuff. If you are so independent that you don't need me, I will find someone who does. It's like this: I know you don't need me to open the door for you, but you are much more attractive when you let me get it.

Girls, **we don't have to be weak.** We don't even have to be incompetent. We just have to pretend like once in a while we *need* a guy. Even if we don't. 'Cuz guys need to be needed. They need to be allowed to be the stronger one, the tougher one, the braver one. **It's a self-trip to think that you can do it all yourself.** You weren't made that way. Your God made

73

you to be part of a community, a large group of people who help one another. And a community filled with people who are unwilling to say "Help" or to allow others to do stuff for them is a dysfunctional community.

It's like this. We are all made to serve one another (Gal. 5:13). Right? But if I never allow you to serve me, then I never allow you to fulfill the command of God on your life. **The epitome of selfishness is to say, "I can do it *all* myself."** Guys get pleasure out of doing things for you. Not everything, but guy things. When we take that chance away from them, we take a piece of their manhood. And we say that guys are irrelevant.

The sexual revolution had its whack at destroying the relationship between men and women. As believers we now have the chance to restore that. **Find out what God planned for guys and girls** and start acting more like the girl God created—tender, soft, gentle, and lovable. 1 Corinthians 11:11. Get the good book out. Look up this verse and write it down here.

• _____

_____

_____

Heavy Lifting

Now it's time for the rubber to hit the road. **If you think you are girl enough, then here is your assignment. This week be a girl.** When a guy is around, let him be a guy. Seems obvious, but not so much. Slow down before you get to the door so he can open it. If you have to carry something, ask him if he would mind doing it for you. Don't roll your eyes at this—we have to give guys their purpose back, even if it's on small stuff. And believe me, they will love it (if they are real men!). **In everything you do, think feminine. Think girly.** Think, *Would he like to do this for me?* Ask him to open your water bottle

74

or the ketchup. **It's true that you don't need him to do things for you.** You are woman enough. But in the old days we needed them to kill the wildebeest, and now that doesn't really apply, so we ask them to open the spaghetti jar. It's not as cool as asking them to kill your dinner for you, but it maintains the balance of male/female power.

So need him this week. Need the male species. Stop competing with them and making them obsolete. Give them a purpose, even if it's just a small one. Let them be men. It will make their day.

A *Dateable* Girl

never gives up

cares about other people as much as herself

doesn't want what she doesn't have

doesn't show off

doesn't have a big head

never forces herself on others

isn't all about being first

doesn't get all angry for stupid stuff

doesn't keep score of her friends' mistakes

doesn't love it when other people beg her for

   forgiveness or attention

loves the truth

is easy to get along with

doesn't complain

always trusts God

always looks for the best

doesn't worry about the past

keeps going toward her goal

(Check out 1 Corinthians 13 for more about the *Dateable* Girl.)

The DATE

WHO DOES WHAT?

by Hastin Morgadoo and Juyley hookagan—the Alligator Hunters

In the *Dateable* kingdom live two integral yet different members of the species: the male, who is the aggressor, the hunter, the provider; and the female, who is the nurturer, the talker, the emoter. The *Dateable* ecosystem needs one male and one female of the species for successful dating.

To help you better understand the *Dateable* ecosystem, we have provided in the pages to follow a thorough breakdown of the dating ritual between male and female human beings. Readers will kindly note that any description of the reader is purely coincidental, as we are investigating the species in general. So without further ado, we have the *Dateable* kingdom.

The Double Take

When the female of the species attempts to attract a mate, the first and most important action is the double take. This is when the male and female see one another and are so alarmed by each other's beauty that they look away in embarrassment but must look back again because the attraction is so strong. The double take is a surefire sign that the male is interested in the female. And the female can let the male see her double take as a nifty clue to alert the male to her interest. But the female must be careful not to overdo it, or the male will feel "played." Thus a subtle look, then a gentle movement of the eyes back down to the ground, a 3-second pause, and then the returning of her

76

gentle eyes to the prey, er, I mean, *male* will further spark his interest if he is indeed interested at all.

THE CLUES

If the male shows interest by returning the female's gentle stare with a smile or an eye lock, then the female can proceed to gently give him more clues to her affection over the next few weeks. The seasoned female will allow herself to be in the view of her target male several times throughout the day. She will make sure to look like she just "happened" to be in his vicinity. She might smile at him, giggle, or even say "hi," but she will never corner him and ask him for a date or talk his ear off. This would be a sign that the female is needy, and it will chase the male away.

Note: If the male shows absolutely no interest in any of the female's clues, then the successful female stops the process here. She knows that to chase a male is not her role as a female, so she moves herself away from the temptation.

The Phone Call

When the healthy male discovers that the female is interested in him, he then steps up to the plate and makes the next advance: the phone call. When the female receives this phone call, she is polite, open, and inquisitive. She asks him questions about his life and pretends to be interested even if she isn't. She doesn't tell him anything negative about her life. She is a delight to talk with, so delightful that when at the end of 10 minutes she says, "Gosh it was nice talking with you, but I have to run," the male hangs up the phone and continues to think about her. She leaves the male wanting more. If the male had enough guts to ask her out, then the *Dateable* girl prepares herself for the date.

Special Note on Availability: The *Dateable* female is a rare gem, a priceless stone, a temple of great value. Therefore she is not easy to get. She is expensive, she is challenging, she is hard to find. And as such she is not available at the spur of the

77

moment for a date. If the male should call on Friday to ask her out for Saturday, she is to be flattered but busy. She tells him she would love to, but she is doing something that night, maybe another time. Now, some untrained observers may object to this by saying, "But she's not doing anything Saturday night." However, the *Dateable* female is *always* doing something. She may be watching TV, washing her hair, or hanging out at home, but she is always doing *something*.

The female who chooses to disregard this piece of advice should get used to becoming the "booty call," the girl he calls when he has no other girl to call. The last-minute date. The for-sure deal. The she'll-do-for-now. But the *Dateable* female wants to be a challenge. She believes in the mystery of a woman, so she teaches him to call her in advance. Like a fine restaurant, she requires reservations at least 4 days prior. She is popular (even if it's only with her mom and dad), and he needs to know that.

The Date

To make it easier for the nonspecialist in the field to understand the next phase of the dating ritual, we have included a list of rules that better explain the Date. Male-female outings in the *Dateable* kingdom must follow these strict rules.

Rule #1: Whoever asks, drives. The smart female knows that the male is the aggressor. He asks, he pays, he drives, he leads. So the smart female allows him to pick her up even if it is out of his way. She never offers to meet him, because she knows that the male loves to work for things. And the harder he works, the more he likes her.

Note: If he isn't old enough to drive, he isn't old enough to date.

Habitat Side Note: If subjects live in a major city with public transportation, the male goes directly to the door to pick up the female and never makes her meet him at the station. He returns her to said location at the end of the outing.

Rule #2: Dateable females don't touch doors. The *Dateable* female doesn't rush to the door; she slows down as they approach it and allows the male time to get in front of her to open the door for her. Then she enters before him and says, "Thank you."

Rule #3: Dateable females aren't picky, but they also know what they want. They don't complain about the restaurant he

78

has chosen, but if it is McDonald's, they might joke about his choice of cuisine as they enjoy their time. She is thankful and appreciative of all his efforts, even his weak ones. "Thank you" is continually heard throughout this ritual.

Rule #4: Whoever asks, pays. The hunter-gatherer male is fulfilled when he is allowed to hunt and gather with his wallet for the female of his dreams. The *Dateable* female does not take this gift away from the male, even if she disagrees with the rule. She knows that if it's a rule, it must be right.

> Note: If he is not fulfilled by this part of the ritual, then he is not man enough to date her.

Rule #5: The *Dateable* female does not kiss him good night, nor give him a touch of her body. She remembers that what is hard to get is attractive—diamond, attractive; pebble, stepped on. She is unique. She is different. She is hard to get.

The Next Day

The truly *Dateable* female refrains from calling the male after the date. Even though she is dying to talk with him, she knows that to call him would upset the male mating ritual. Instead she occupies her time with friends and family and attempts not to ponder the date to extremes. She knows that if the male is the mate for her, he will attempt further contact. And if not, then she won't become angry.

As we have shown, the seasoned *Dateable* female understands the behavior and rituals of the male of the species. She isn't so self-absorbed as to ignore his needs in the dating ritual. She respects his need to be needed, his passion for the chase, and his fear of suffocation. She is available, yet not too available. She is the perfect prize, the confident female. He will pursue her to the ends of the kingdom if indeed she is a *Dateable* female.

79

It's Date Night again. My, how time flies, huh? So what shall we do tonight? Maybe dinner and a movie? That's a bit more traditional than last week. Or is it? Here's Part 1: food. Doesn't have to be fancy, just has to be a place where they seat you and serve you. Your first job is to be confident. Your second job is to love people. And that means your server, the busboy, whoever you come into contact with. What does loving them mean? It means care about them. Treat them like humans. Treat them like God's precious kids. How? Here are some pointers:

- Find out their name and tell them yours. You are, after all, all God's kids. They aren't your slaves.
- Respect the fact that they have a hard job, and give them a break.
- Be friendly. Care about them.
- Don't get upset if they get your food wrong or late. (Note: You can certainly say something, but not in an angry way.)
- Smile at them.
- Leave them a big tip. (You don't have to do this every time. Just muster all you can today and do it. Did you know that Christians are known in the food industry as the worst tippers? That means that servers hate serving Christians. You are God's representative. Represent him as best you can. Be generous. Don't tell them it's from Jesus; just love them like Jesus would. Their spirits will know, and their hearts will be lifted.)

Part 2: after dinner, a movie. For this, pick a movie that might actually have a substantial plot. Something besides the sequel to *American Pie* or anything Tom Green. Maybe a remake of an old film. Or a drama. Historical movies are great. Even a great

animated film would be good, since they are loaded with content. If you want to try a rental, then here are some good ones to start with: *Bruce Almighty, Finding Nemo, The Count of Monte Cristo, The Matrix, Shrek, Gladiator, The Shawshank Redemption, The Hurricane, Signs, Dead Man Walking.*

Your goal: Find Jesus in the film. After the film, go to a coffee shop or back home and talk about your thoughts on the spiritual impact of the film. If you can't find a symbol of Jesus or his life, then find the biblical message. Every film has one. **God is everywhere there is substance.** If you can't find God in the film, then find where it's missing God. Ask questions like this:

- What was the moral?
- Was there any faith in the characters' lives? What was their faith in?
- How did they try to control their happiness?
- What was their fatal flaw that would keep them from Christ?
- How did they resemble a believer?
- What was missing from their lives (besides the obvious answer of Christ)?
- What did they need more than anything to lead them to Christ?
- How did their sin keep them in turmoil?
- How would a relationship with Christ have changed their lives?
- If God wasn't real to the characters, then why? What kept them separate from him?

That should get you going. Spend a good 30 minutes talking about the movie. Find God in it. Find him in as much of the movie as you can. And don't ever miss God in anything. He is everywhere. Everything points back to him.

Yee haw! You made it through the month and have become the most *Dateable* person on the planet. It's time to par-tay! Hopefully you've been working on this for 3 weeks and you are cranked and ready to go! But here's a little recap of what this *Dateable* Bash will involve:

Quiz Your *Dateability*

Walk Down Memory Lane – news report, slide show, photo album, lots of laughs

Awards Ceremony – the good, the better, the totally *Dateable*

Fun – eat, talk, laugh, have a ball

First things first! Now, just to find out how far you've come on the *Dateable* journey, we've got a parting quiz for you. Let's see if you've really learned anything at all. Take it—that is, if you aren't too scared of failing!

QUIZ: What Do You Know about Guys Now?

1. When it comes to asking a guy out, I:
   a. still think it's my prerogative
   b. would rather wait to see if he gets my hints
   c. make it easy for him and tell his friend to tell him to call me

2. The last time I was with a guy, I:
   a. talked his ear off, and boy did it feel good
   b. talked about fun stuff; we had a great conversation
   c. let him talk (and I almost fell asleep, but he seemed to really want to talk)

3. Which term best describes guys?
   a. shoppers
   b. hunters
   c. jerks

82

4. Which statement would a guy rather hear at the end of a date?
    a. "You have great eyes."
    b. "The food was terrible."
    c. "I loved the movie."

5. If he asks, he pays.   True   False

6. If he's not old enough to drive, he's not old enough to ask me out.   True   False

7. I am a confident girl.   True   False

8. When I am talking to someone, I always look them in the eye.   True   False

9. Guys prefer:
    a. mystery
    b. communication
    c. help

10. When a guy calls me, I:
    a. talk on the phone as long as I can, the longer the better
    b. let him decide when to hang up—he's the guy, after all
    c. hang up after 15 minutes. I'm a busy girl

Scoring:

1. a = 3, b = 1, c = 2
2. a = 3 , b = 1, c = 3
3. a = 3, b = 1, c = 3
4. a = 2, b = 3, c = 1
5. True = 1, False = 3

6. True = 1, False = 3
7. True = 1, False = 3
8. True = 1, False = 3
9. a = 1, b = 2, c = 3
10. a = 3, b = 2, c = 1

10–15: Dear *Dateable* Grad, *you did it! You read the book, you passed the class, and you're ready to go on to Dateable Greatness. Your love life should be pure perfection, or at least a heck of a lot better than it used to be. Good job!*

16–20: Almost *Dateable*. *Well, what can I say? You read the book. You did the focus groups. You had the dates. But still not too sure it really all makes sense? That's okay. Give it some time. Read the book again. Try out some of the stuff we suggest. Results will come; it's just a matter of time.*

21–30: Did you read the same book? *Where did we go wrong? Did you remember to read the girls' side and not the guys'? Maybe take another trip down* Dateable *Lane. A second read might do you good. Or heck, just keep doing what you've been doing—you're sure to keep getting what you've been getting!*

Once you've done the Quiz, you can party on with all the other cool stuff you planned. Save the serious business, "Commit to the List," to do later on your own. This is the time to let loose and enjoy the success of a hard journey. Yep, guys are still impossible to understand. And you will still feel inadequate at times, but now you understand a little more about what is *really* going in the guy/girl world.

If you've loved this *Dateable* month and the way you've grown with your group, then keep the feeling alive. Plan a "Dinner at 8" once a month. What's that, you say? Glad you asked. You're so good like that. Dinner at 8 is just what it sounds like. It's dinner and it's at 7:00 (just kidding, it really is at 8:00). Get your gang together once a month and go out. Let the guys plan something fun. Let them open doors and pull out chairs. Thank them for all they've done. Be *Dateable!* It's a blast! If you're committing to do this, then get on **www.RUDateable.com** and let us know. We'd love to find out what's going on and how your Dinner at 8 works. We also want photos. You can submit your photos from your *Dateable* Bash newscast and any other photos you shoot from then on. We'll keep the rest of the world posted on your *Dateable* journey!

84

On Your Own — The Solo Wrap-Up

Commit to the List

It's time to really get serious about who you are as a *Dateable* Girl. Make the *Dateable* attitude a part of who you are—"Commit to the List."

This commitment is between you and your God. He knows what is in your heart, and he will help you stick to your commitment. So after you read the list of *Dateable* Rules and agree with them, in the space given write him a prayer that tells him why you want to Commit to the List. Be sure to sign it. That's your word. Then your job, besides staying committed, is to tell at least one other person about your *Dateable* commitment. This puts you on the right path for becoming who God wants you to be.

The Dateable *Rules* (For Girls)

1. Accept Your Girlyness – You're a girl. Be proud of all that means. You are soft, you are gentle, you are woman. Don't try to be a guy. Guys like you because you are different from them. So let your girlyness soar.

2. Tell It Like It Is – *Dateable* girls don't lie to themselves. They don't say stuff like, "His girlfriend just isn't good to him—that's why he's seeing me on the side," or "She started it, so I'm going to get even." The *Dateable* girl lets God run the world and tells herself the truth, that all she can control is herself. She doesn't imagine things to be more than they are.

3. The Sexiest Thing on a Girl Is Happiness – Girls try so hard to add beauty and sexuality to themselves with clothes and makeup, but the truth is that it's your spirit

85

that makes you hot. Your outlook on life, your happiness factor. *Dateable* girls aren't downers. They love life.

4. Girls Don't Fight Other Girls—Ever – Revenge belongs to God. *Dateable* girls know that when they fight other girls, they look stupid and catty, and guys don't like it any more than God does.

5. Believe in Your Beauty – *Dateable* girls learn how to overcome the stuff people did to them in the past. They don't let the enemy steal their beauty. God made them, so they know they are beautiful, even if they don't feel like it sometimes.

6. Be Mysterious – *Dateable* girls know how to shut up. They don't monopolize the conversation. They don't tell everyone everything about themselves. They save some for later. They listen more than they gab.

7. Act Confident – *Dateable* girls know that confidence is hot. And the cool part is that no one knows if you are confident but you. Confidence isn't how you feel; it's how you act. Act confident and people will think you are.

8. Look 'Em in the Eye – Part of being a *Dateable* girl is really seeing people. People matter, but if you don't look them in the eye, then you will never really see them, and they will never know they matter to you. Look 'em in the eye because they are valuable.

9. Let Him Lead – God made guys to be leaders. *Dateable* girls get that and let him do guy things like get the door and open the ketchup bottle. They relax and let guys be guys. Which means they don't ask him out!

10. Need Him – *Dateable* girls know that guys need to be needed. A *Dateable* girl isn't Miss Independent. She knows we are made for community. Needing each other is part of faith. She allows him to be needed at times, knowing he was called to serve just as much as she was.

86

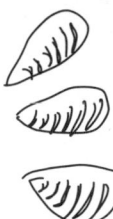

If you agree with the Rules, you are ready to Commit to the List. Here it is:

As a *Dateable* girl, I will:

1. shut up and be mysterious
2. not lie to myself
3. keep it covered up
4. remember that I'm not one of the guys
5. know that it will not last

Dear God,

_____

_____

_____

_____

_____

_____

_____

_____

_____

_____
Name